D1458681

# GEN!US

# PEARSON

At Pearson, we believe in learning – all kinds of learning for all kinds of people. Whether it's at home, in the classroom or in the workplace, learning is the key to improving our life chances.

That's why we're working with leading authors to bring you the latest thinking and the best practices, so you can get better at the things that are important to you. You can learn on the page or on the move, and with content that's always crafted to help you understand quickly and apply what you've learned.

If you want to upgrade your personal skills or accelerate your career, become a more effective leader or more powerful communicator, discover new opportunities or simply find more inspiration, we can help you make progress in your work and life.

Pearson is the world's leading learning company. Our portfolio includes the Financial Times, Penguin, Dorling Kindersley, and our educational business, Pearson International.

Every day our work helps learning flourish, and wherever learning flourishes, so do people.

To learn more please visit us at: **www.pearson.com/uk**

# GEN!US

## Deceptively simple ways to become instantly smarter

## James Bannerman

PEARSON

Harlow, England • London • New York • Boston • San Francisco • Toronto • Sydney
Auckland • Singapore • Hong Kong • Tokyo • Seoul • Taipei • New Delhi
Cape Town • São Paulo • Mexico City • Madrid • Amsterdam • Munich • Paris • Milan

Pearson Education Limited

Edinburgh Gate
Harlow CM20 2JE
Tel: +44 (0)1279 623623
Fax: +44 (0)1279 431059
Website: www.pearson.com/uk

First published in Great Britain in 2012

© James Bannerman 2012

The right of James Bannerman to be identified as author of this work has
been asserted by him in accordance with the Copyright, Designs and Patents
Act 1988.

Pearson Education is not responsible for the content of third-party internet sites.

ISBN: 978-0-273-77226-2

British Library Cataloguing-in-Publication Data
A catalogue record for this book is available from the British Library

Library of Congress Cataloging-in-Publication Data
Bannerman, James.
  Genius! : deceptively simple ways to become instantly smarter / James
Bannerman.
    p. cm.
  ISBN 978-0-273-77226-2 (limp)
  1. Genius. 2. Creative ability. 3. Cognition. I. Title.
  BF412.B33 2012
  153.4'2--dc23
                                          2012008815

10 9 8 7 6 5 4 3 2 1
16 15 14 13 12

Text design by Design Deluxe

Typeset in 9.5/14 Helvetica Neue Light by 30
Printed and bound in Great Britain by Henry Ling Ltd., at the Dorset Press,
Dorchester, Dorset

Dedicated to my father – Henry Campbell Bannerman (1931–2010) – who gave me the freedom and opportunity to follow a creative path

And to A, T, and S xxx

# CONTENTS

# ACKNOWLEDGEMENTS

Firstly, I'd like to thank Edward de Bono for the insightful conversations we've had over the years, and whose pioneering work inspired me to write this book.

Secondly, I'd like to thank Rachael Stock, Paul East (and the whole Pearson Team) for being so incredibly upbeat about **The Genius Project** and for helping to make it happen... I genuinely can't thank you enough.

Thirdly, I'd like to thank all of my Department of Business and Management colleagues at Oxford Brookes University for their support and friendship, and for championing 'Innovation, Creativity and Enterprise' well before it became fashionable to do so. In particular, Richard Beresford, Nicolette Michels, Richard Mohun, Phil Morgan, Nigel Bassett-Jones, Dr Louise Grisoni, Dr Karen Handley, Dr David Bowen and Professor Phil James. I'd also like to extend my gratitude to Kathleen Molan at Warwick Business School, Phil Eyre at Grenoble Ecole de Management, Roger Neill at Cass, Professors Richard Jolly and John Bates at LBS, and Professor Roger Mumby-Croft who helped to start the ball rolling.

Finally, I'd like to thank a range of 'unsung heroes' who helped me more than they probably realise: Andy Harries, Rebecca Frayn, Simon Woodroffe, Hossein Amini, Andrew Farish, Charlie Beauchamp, Julian Marc Stringle, Berny and Di Stringle, Giles Gibbons, Dr Juliet Williams, Philippa Thomas, Laura Whitworth, Carol Fisher, Claire Watmore, Paddy Thompson, Louise Davies,

Henry Berry, Paul Birch, Roland Stringer, Simon Napier-Bell, Phil de Glanville and Guy Browning.

And, of course, family and friends for always being there.

# ABOUT THE AUTHOR

## James Bannerman
*Creative Change Agent*

**James Bannerman** is a Creative
Change Agent who combines
creativity with psychology to help
businesses innovate.

As an Innovation Consultant he
has worked with many leading
organisations including British
Airways, Orange, Starbucks,
Rolls-Royce and HSBC, as well
as at the National Space Centre
on a mission to Mars. He also lectures on business creativity and
innovation on the MBA programmes at Warwick Business School,
Grenoble Ecole de Management and Oxford Brookes University,
where he is currently doing a PhD on the impact of lateral thinking
upon organisational performance.

Before working in business he was a platinum-selling
songwriter, a freelance cartoonist (e.g. *Punch*), a trained clinical
psychotherapist, and he has an MA Hons in English Literature
from Edinburgh University.

# AUTHOR'S NOTE

**GENIUS!** = Skilled in inventing or thinking out new ideas

'd love to say I wrote this book because I am a genius, but I'm not.

I'd also love to say I have a guru's gift for transforming anyone who reads it into a genius, too, but I don't.

Oddly enough, that's not what this book is about.

It's *not* about turning you into the next Shakespeare, Pelé, Marie Curie or Beethoven (fantastic though that might be). What it *is* about is helping you to develop your **Genius Thinking Skills** so you can have more **Genius Moments** in both your personal and professional life. In other words, it's about introducing you to a variety of practical tools and techniques for triggering those amazing 'aha' moments when you…

➜ Think your way out of a tricky situation

➜ Fix that challenging issue you've been longing to fix

➜ Spot commercial opportunities that others fail to spot

➜ Create 'something out of nothing' in an enriching and enterprising way.

Evidence suggests that if we want to survive and thrive in a rapidly changing world we need to develop our **Inner Genius**: we need to be able to solve problems in ways others wouldn't think of, generate brilliant ideas, persuade people in ingenious ways, and tweak something ordinary and make it special.

In other words, those who are able to think creatively now have a massive advantage – in the workplace and at home. And everyone can do it, with a bit of help. This deceptively simple book can show you how...

# INTRODUCTION

The aim of this book is simple. It is designed to help you develop your **Genius Thinking Skills**.

Why?

Because, unfortunately, in business and life, 'success' is not always about how hard you think or how hard you work: it's about how 'smart' you think, and how 'smart' you work... and that's why **Genius Thinking** is so important. Here are three quick examples to remind us why:

## A GENIUS HELPED DAVID BEAT GOLIATH

Goliath was a nine-foot giant (so they say) and far too big, strong and scary for anyone to conquer in hand-to-hand combat. But then along came a young boy called David with a **Genius Idea**.

It didn't involve sharp swords, long spears, or even heavy body armour. Nope. That would have been far too predictable and, let's face it, worryingly naïve against such a mammoth man-monster.

So what did David do ?

Well, he used a **Genius Twist of Thought**. As author Shiva Khera points out, he stopped thinking that Goliath was 'too big to hit', and started thinking that he was 'too big to miss'. He simply bent down, picked up some pebbles, placed one of them in a catapult, and then aimed it right between Goliath's eyes. End of story, or at least it was for Goliath.

## B GENIUS HELPED ELIOT NESS NAIL AL CAPONE

Back in the 1920s the FBI found it nigh on *impossible* to arrest the Godfather of all Godfathers, Al Capone.

**AL CAPONE**

Even though his criminal empire was involved with every kind of crime imaginable – from murder to illegal booze smuggling, and bribery to extortion – who could prove it? Al Capone was so powerful that even members of the police and judicial system would rather take his money than take him on and, besides, his super-intelligent lawyers could easily run rings around anyone who dared to make such 'criminal' accusations.

So how did they catch him?

Well, once again, the solution didn't involve them tackling the problem head-on; it involved **obliquity** and coming at the tough problem from an unexpected angle. Treasury Agent Eliot Ness and his cunningly clever team of Untouchables managed to nab him because of… tax evasion!

In other words, they deliberately side-stepped *predictable solutions* and asked themselves why it was that Capone – who had huge assets – appeared to have no legitimate source of income. Amazingly, Capone had *never* paid tax. Consequently, because they discovered this cunning loophole, Capone was finally found guilty in a U.S. court of law and spent the rest of his days locked up behind iron bars on the island of Alcatraz.

## C GENIUS CREATED THE DALEK (WITHOUT COSTING THE EARTH)

In 1963 Ray Cusick – a special effects expert working at the BBC – was given the challenge of creating a new outer-space character called a Dalek based upon an idea by screenwriter Terry Nation. The trouble was that he

**DALEK (1963)**

had only one tenth of the budget he would have ideally wanted. He simply didn't have the money to do all the things he would have loved to do, so he used a little **Cunningly Clever Creativity** (a big part of **Genius Thinking**) and improvised.

As a result, he cobbled together all kinds of inexpensive household items, from a sink-plunger to an egg whisk (and even a pepper shaker) to create an iconic alien which once upon a time had nervous children jumping behind their sofa for safety the second it appeared on their TV screens…

## THE METHOD IN THE MADNESS

'OK', you might well be saying to yourself, 'So what? I still can't see how exploring the world of giants, gangsters and aliens, is supposed to help *me* improve *my* life?'

Here's how.

Whatever challenges you currently face in life – whether they be as tiny as curing annoying hiccups or as awkward as striking a better work–life balance – you basically have two options:

Your first option is to zap it with a *known solution*. If this works, great. Forget about **Genius** (and while you're at it ditch the idea of thinking about giants, gangsters and aliens too).

Alternatively, if all you want to do is *toast a piece of bread*, for example, coming up with wacky ideas involving fire-eating dragons or roller-skate volcanoes might be inventive, but it's also likely to be a poor use of your precious time and energy. Far better to opt for the *tried-and-tested* toaster like everyone else (which **Genius** Maddy Kennedy invented back in 1872).

In reality, however, not all problems in life are as easy to fix as toasting a piece of bread (and, let's face it, life would be pretty dull if they were).

For instance:

→ Maybe you're facing a new type of problem you haven't encountered before

→ Maybe life's 'goalposts' have shifted and the 'old' solutions don't work any more

→ Maybe there is no 'known solution'

→ Maybe there is, but you've absolutely no idea where to find it.

# WHAT THEN?

Well, that's when the second option – **The Genius Option** – can start to become mega-useful.

It's when we come to realise that, in order to make progress, and stop banging our heads against the same old brick wall, we need to step beyond the *usual* and explore the *unusual* – as David did with Goliath, Eliot Ness did with Al Capone, and Ray Cusick did with the Dalek.

This doesn't mean that **Genius Thinking** holds the key to fixing *all* of your life's challenges. Of course not. All it means is that if you're ever feeling 'stuck', and the familiar solutions aren't getting you anywhere, a stroke of imaginative genius can often come in handy, as we're about to discover...

---

**'Discovery consists of looking at the same thing as everyone else and thinking something different.'**

Albert Szent-Gyorgy (the Genius Nobel-Prize winner who discovered vitamin C)

---

# HOW TO GET THE BEST OUT OF THIS BOOK

This book is a veritable treasure trove of specific mindtools and techniques for helping you to tap into your **Inner Genius** – or what Benjamin Franklin once called 'the silver in the mine' – so you can solve problems more quickly, tackle issues with sparkling brilliance and generally achieve greater success in your work and your personal life.

In Genius at Work, on p.77 you'll find a complete toolkit of approaches to business issues. Please feel free to skip to that section right now if it's *specifically* creative business solutions you're after today.

Before that, we're going to tackle two issues in one.

**1** It might be quite good to be a genius generally, rather than just at work. You see, **Genius Thinking** is great for solving all kinds of niggly little everyday problems – and some huge life-crunching ones, too. That's got to be appealing.

**2** If we're honest, most of us are hoping for a fast-track, high-speed, cut-to-the-chase version of pretty much everything. There's always a place for 'right here, right now' results.

So, if you want a 'right here, right now' guide for boosting your genius and/or would like to know how to apply **Genius Thinking** to absolutely any issue, from everyday domestic niggles to big work crises, read straight on.

First stop, it's welcome to the weird and wonderful world of CUNNING CAN**DO**…

# INSTANT GENIUS

Aka CUNNING CAN**DO**

The 5 essential Cunningly Clever Tools for
fixing everyday challenges – big or small

'Millions saw the apple
fall but Newton was the
one who asked why.'
Bernard Baruch

Later in this book you will be introduced to 26 different mindtools for stimulating your own **Genius Ideas**. Here, we're going to be focusing on just a smaller selection of tools and applying them to a very broad range of situations. It's the fast-track guide to **Genius Thinking**, for those of us who need to know the secrets instantly, and who need a touch of genius in all areas of our lives.

So, if it's **Snappy Genius** you're after, stay right here. CUNNING CAN**DO** will quickly introduce you to the 5 principle ways for helping you to generate new ideas, whatever the situation, whatever the context.

If it's **Spready Genius** you're after, however, in terms of a much wider selection of tools for your toolbox, then you might want to keep on reading, or turn now to p. 93.

# CUNNING CANDO

**'Everything is possible.**
**The impossible just takes longer.'**

Dan Brown (Author of *The Da Vinci Code*)

If you were to take all the creative thinking tools and techniques in the world and then distil them down to just 5, and only 5, these would be those 5...

**C**UNNING **C**ONNECTIONS
**C**UNNING **A**LTERATIONS
**C**UNNING **N**AVIGATIONS
**C**UNNING **D**IRECTIONS
**C**UNNING **O**PPOSITIONS

In a moment we'll be exploring what they actually mean and, more importantly, in what ways you can use them to help you fix all kinds of little problems, and BIG problems, in your life.

Before we begin, however, you may be wondering what we mean by CUNNING and by CAN**DO**. Let's start with CAN**DO**.

# CANDO

Evidence suggests that genius, like success, comes in **CANS** not in **CAN-NOTS**.

This is why many geniuses throughout history – from commercial geniuses to artistic geniuses and even political geniuses – have done their best to highlight the importance of a CAN**DO** attitude:

→ 'If you think you can do a thing or think you can't do a thing, you're right.' *(Henry Ford)*

→ 'He can who thinks he can, and he can't who thinks he can't.' *(Pablo Picasso)*

→ 'Nurture the mind with great thoughts, for you will never go any higher than you think.' *(Benjamin Disraeli)*

It's also why we tend to think of the CAN**DO** Mozart as a genius rather than the **CAN'T DO** Emperor Joseph II, who famously told Wolfgang his music had 'too many notes'!

Or why we think of the CAN**DO** Wright Brothers as geniuses for inventing the first ever plane to fly in 1903, rather more than the **CAN'T DO** astronomer Simon Newcomb who sceptically pointed out in 1902 that, 'Flight by machines heavier than air is impractical and insignificant, if not utterly impossible.'

And so, at the end of the day, one could deduce that, if you want more **Genius Moments** in your life, here's the secret:

Create a life for yourself where there are more squiggles and fewer straight lines. Why? Because…

Non-**Genius** minds are full of statements and exclamation marks:

'I can't afford it!'

'It can't possibly work!'

'This problem can't be fixed!'

**Genius** minds are full of explorations and question marks:

'How can I afford it?'

'How can I potentially get it to work?'

'In what other ways can I look at this problem to help me fix it?'

Admittedly, it sounds pretty obvious, but (as we'll discover later) genius doesn't always have to be complicated.

Yet before we move on to the CUNNING bit, there are two additional reasons why CAN**DO** was deliberately, rather than accidentally, chosen for this part.

Firstly, it could be argued that the tin can (invented by Peter Durand in 1810) is a powerful visual symbol of what **Genius** is all about. After all, this genius invention helped to revolutionise the way food was preserved and transported around the globe. In fact, Ezra Warner's invention of a tin can opener was possibly an even better idea, but that didn't come along until over 40 years later!

Secondly, it might be worth considering how even a very old, very naff, and very overused cliché like the CAN**DO** cliché can also have one good thing going for it: clichés are easy to remember.

And memorability is important, especially if you want the mindtools in this book to benefit you as much as possible in your day-to-day life.

Right. Now we've got that out the way, what about the CUNNING bit?

## WHY CUNNING?

Well, George Bernard Shaw might well have said, 'You see things and you say "Why?" But I dream things that never were and I say "Why not?"' But he was a bit of a pompous genius, so let's forget about him.

Here's the real answer.

CUNNING is without doubt a strange word.

On the one hand we associate it with being rather sly and deceitful like a wily fox, a Machiavellian politician, Dickens's Artful Dodger, or, worst of all... a second-hand car salesman.

On the other, we often secretly admire 'cunning minds' for their amazing ability to think laterally and step around the very problems that 'fox' the rest of us.

This book is aimed solely at the second category, or what could potentially be called *ethical cunning*. It is *not* about encouraging you to be 'dodgy' in business or life, or to trample on others in a ruthless pursuit of personal or professional success. Far from it.

It *is* about showing you how, in order to have more of the **Genius Moments** we mentioned earlier, we often need to learn the art of being **Cunningly Clever**...

So here goes. And if at times you find **Cunningly Clever Creativity** rather childlike, fantastic! The more childlike the better...

---

**'The secret of genius is to carry the spirit of childhood into maturity.'**
T.H. Huxley

---

The first CUNNING CAN**DO** technique you can use to help you fix life's tricky problems is **Cunning Connections** (also known as 'Bisociation' as we'll discuss later).

The good news is that it's fairly easy to use. All you have to do is ask yourself the following question: 'What might happen if I *connected this* with *that* to create something new?' For example, here's how others have experimented with unusual *connections* in the past to come up with all kinds of fresh concepts and clever inventions:

> *Connect* tin with copper, and what do you get?... *Bronze*
>
> *Connect* a woman with a fish? ... *A mermaid*
>
> *Connect* breakfast and lunch? ... *Brunch*
>
> *Connect* sawdust with glue? ... *Chipboard/MDF*
>
> *Connect* the sail of a tiny boat with a surfboard? ... *Windsurfing*

Yup. Virtually everywhere you look the chances are you'll begin to see evidence of **Cunning Connections Genius** at work, from a patchwork quilt to wallpaper, a radio-alarm clock to Gin & Tonic, and Teenage Mutant Ninja Turtles to a supermarket (which, let's face it, is nothing more than loads of different shops merged together under one roof from a butcher to a baker, and a green-grocer to a newsagent).

So why not have a go at looking at one of your own day-to-day problems, and then – like an octopus reaching out in all directions – imagine what might happen if you could suddenly mix and match it with something different or unexpected. Please don't expect instant miracles, however, simply have a go and see where it takes you... After all, these days we might not view muesli as being particularly innovative, but once upon a time (1900 to be precise) it all started when a Swiss scientist called

Dr Bircher-Benner asked the question 'What if I *connected* and combined whole oats with fruit and grains and milk and a few other bits and pieces?' And how nuts was that?

## CUNNING CONNECTIONS DOODLE..

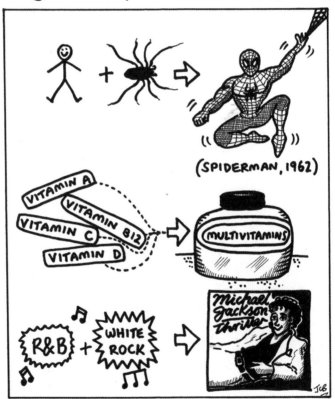

**O**ne of the most amazing **Genius** *connectors* of all time was *John Logie Baird* (the inventor of the TV).

Back in the 1920s, in the English seaside town of Hastings, Baird began experimenting away with all kinds of weird and wonderful apparatus to create a moving picture machine. These included the following:

**A cardboard disc cut from a hat box + a tin plate cut out with scissors + lenses from bicycle lamps + sealing wax + darning needles for spindles + a small electric fan motor + tea chests and many other little bits and pieces along the way. (source: www.1066.net/baird)**

Subsequently, of course, other cunningly clever brains have *connected* additional elements to TV and film, too, adding colour to black and white, and also an extra dimension to 2D to give us 3D and now even 4D, too...

## CUNNING CONNECTIONS
## TURNING THEORY INTO PRACTICE

OK. Enough theory? Now comes the important part. Sure, we might get the point that loads of inventions and solutions to problems come from combining things we often wouldn't necessarily think of combining (such as sugar and vinegar to cure hiccups), but so what? Let's look at how the same underlying principle of **Cunning Connections** can potentially help *you* in your life.

The point is that it's about thinking differently. It's about shaking the tree, not trimming the hedge! It's about using a provocative technique for stimulating ideas you probably wouldn't have come up with any other way. By asking yourself, 'What could I add in

here that I would never normally think of adding in?' you will start to use your brain in a totally new way.

A quick aside: before you set about experimenting with new *connections*, however, please ensure that you *keep yourself safe* and *others safe* at all times when applying any of the tools and techniques in this book. Yes, I know this sounds a bit over-parental and Health-and-Safetyish, but it's genuinely important: connect *saltpetre + charcoal + sulphur*, for example – as **Genius** Chinese alchemists did around AD 800 – and there's a good chance you'll have enough gunpowder to fly off into space like a firework!

Similarly, as any lover of D.I.Y. would point out, go easy when connecting *sand + gravel + limestone + water* (as the **Genius** Romans did to help build arches, domes and vaults) or you could end up knee-deep in concrete. So *please please please* go easy, and only focus on **Cunning Connections** that help you to make your personal life better, not worse. Some *connections* can be lovably harmless, rather like a big fluffy St Bernard's Dog which is basically a *mastiff* + a *Great Dane* + a *mountain dog from the Pyrenees.* Other *connections*, however, can sometimes go awry, as Dr Frankenstein knew only too well…

## CUNNING CONNECTIONS FOR FIXING LIFE'S LITTLE PROBLEMS

**PROBLEM A** How can I separate two cups that have accidentally got stuck together?

**CUNNINGLY CLEVER SOLUTION** *Connect* cold water and hot water

**I**f pure and naked brute force is likely to chip or damage your precious kitchen cups, simply put the bottom cup in a container of boiling hot water, and then pour ice cold water into the top cup. This expand/contract effect should be enough to prise them apart.

**PROBLEM B** How can I loosen the lid on this overtight jam jar?

**CUNNINGLY CLEVER SOLUTION** *Connect* the twisting action of your hand with an elastic band.

**M**ore often than not, if you find it tricky to loosen the lid on a jam jar, it's got nothing to do with you being wimpy and weak rather than macho and strong. It's because you need a firmer grip. So have a go at double-folding or triple-folding an elastic band around the outer rim of the lid. That should make it much easier to turn.

# CUNNING CONNECTIONS FOR FIXING LIFE'S BIGGER CHALLENGES

**CHALLENGE C** I don't know what to buy them for a present.

**CUNNINGLY CLEVER SOLUTION** *Connect* different types of presents with a central theme.

**B**uying presents for some people, as you may well have discovered, isn't always easy (especially if they're very fussy or you don't want to end up spending a fortune). Where most people often struggle, however, is finding the 'single' perfect present. If this is true for you, forget about the idea of a *single* present and go for a **Genius** blend instead.

For example, suppose you were planning to give your young niece a book for Christmas and you thought that Charles Dickens's *A Christmas Carol* might be suitably seasonal. Good idea? Well, possibly, but there's also a good chance your niece will look on you as the most boring old Uncle or Aunt on the planet! *Connect* the book with a packet of humbugs, however, and, by the law of averages, at least one of them is likely to put a smile on her face.

## PROBLEM D My memory's shocking and I'm forgetting really important things.

### CUNNINGLY CLEVER SOLUTION *Connect* ordinary information with extraordinary information.

Many of the world's leading memory experts – from Tony Buzan to Dominic O'Brien – tell us that the key to a good memory comes down to 'linkages' and fusing 'imagination' with 'association'. My cousin, for example, used to continually forget his godchild's birthday year-on-year, which happened to be on the 4$^{th}$ of May. So what did he do? He mentally *connected* this ordinary day – which is much like all the other 364 days in the year – to *Star Wars* and ended up with … *'May the 4$^{th}$ be with you'*. He's never forgotten his godchild's birthday since. **Genius**!

 +

## PROBLEM E I don't have enough hours in the day to do everything I need to do.

### CUNNINGLY CLEVER SOLUTION *Connect* tasks you wouldn't normally *connect* together

Time management is a big challenge for many people, largely because it's not really about time.

It's about how we manage ourselves.

This means it's closely linked to our personality type, our values, our 'life scripts', and even the knock-on effect of other people's poor time management issues too. But unfortunately we don't have 'time' to go into this right now.

One tip-top piece of advice time management experts often give, however, is for us to 'cluster' activities we'd normally keep separate.

For example, they suggest we use 'chunking' to make all of our phone calls in one go, or send all of our e-mails in one go, or perhaps even do all of our worrying in one go?

Clearly, this might not *always* be feasible, but sometimes it can help.

I once ran a time management coaching session for a client, for example, who genuinely did worry a lot. His work performance was suffering as a result, and this caused him to worry even more!

But when we actually sat down to work out how much time he spent worrying in the average week the figures were quite staggering. It was at least an hour a day, and often a couple of hours each night too because he wasn't sleeping very well. In other words, without realising it, he was wasting over eight hours a week just worrying!

So we discussed a strategy for him to do all his worrying at a set time – a 'worry hour' or 'worry half-hour', so to speak – when he could write down each and every worry, and then explore practical steps for dealing with them one by one. As a result, he started to feel far more in control, far less stressed, and yes… he even ended up with more hours in his day to do all the things he needed to do.

**S**o there you have it. Whatever personal challenge you might currently be facing in your life, you might find it helpful to explore additional and alternative *connections* you haven't contemplated before. For example, if you're a chemistry teacher who finds it difficult to engage and inspire the 'bored' children in your class, how about combining 'chemistry' with 'dance'? A little odd? Certainly. However, I was once told about a teacher who did precisely this at a school in South Africa. Different children dressed up in different coloured T-shirts (e.g. red for hydrogen and blue for oxygen) and then moved around the room clustering together and then splitting up to form new combinations. Not only was it much more fun and interesting for the kids – rather than 'talk and chalk' and ping-pong balls – but, suddenly, complicated chemistry became much easier to understand!

CONNECTIONS...CONNECTIONS...CONNECTIONS

ADRIAN DALSEY
LARRY HILLBLOM
ROBERT LYNN ⇨ DHL

HUMPHREY BROTHERS ⇨ UMBRO

PHONE VOICE DATA ⇨ vodafone

KOLA NUT + DIGESTIVE ENZYME (PEPSIN) ⇨ PEPSI-COLA

Also, please note that **Cunning Connections** is the reason why we have everything from seat belts in cars to fluoride in toothpaste. It's even the reason why we have the electric battery (created by Volta in 1800 when he *connected zinc + silver*), and the modern bra! Why? Because many moons ago the **Genius** inventor Mary Phelps Jacob felt that traditional corsets were too uncomfortable to wear and decided to *connect two silk handkerchiefs + a ribbon* as a **Cunningly Clever** alternative.

**BY THE WAY ...** if you're into **Genius** shortcuts for fixing everyday problems, in Japan they call it URAWAZA and there's a useful little book on the subject called *Urawaza* by Liza Katayama which can offer some top tips. For example, if you *connect lemon juice + salt* it can evidentally help you to get rid of the rust on your bicycle...

# AND FINALLY

Next time you feel stuck, here are 3 **Cunning Connections** questions you might want to ask yourself to help you break through the impasse:

❶ What can I potentially *add* to what I'm doing to help fix this problem?

❷ What can I potentially *mix* with this to improve it?

❸ What if I could potentially end up with the best of both worlds?

# THINKSPIRATION
## 'Creativity is just connecting things.'
Steve Jobs (the Genius behind Apple, Pixar, etc....)

The second CUNNING CANDO technique you can use to generate new ideas is to imagine that you're a wizard or magician with the power to transform your problem instantly... 'Just like that!'

Maybe you could use your Harry Potter or Hermione Granger super-skills to *alter* your problem's shape, size, speed, structure, style, shade or sequence (or anything else beginning with the letter S for that matter).

If you're not too sure about this 'abracadbra' approach, however, because it sounds a bit bonkers, please think again. Countless innovations we use today wouldn't exist if **Genius** inventors hadn't taken familiar products and then *altered* them in some way, from soft loo paper to swivel-chairs, reflector sunglasses to extendable hoses, and diet coke to low-fat margarine. For example:

*Altered* coffee has given us everything from instant coffee (which is less hassle to make) to decaffeinated coffee (which won't keep us awake at night) to Fairtrade coffee (which we can drink with a clearer conscience).

Similarly...

*Altered* bicycles have given us everything from the fold-up bicycle (which can help commuters get to work) to the unicycle (which keeps many circus clowns in work) to the mountain bike (which can help over-stressed holidaymakers forget about work).

Yup, the fact is that many things in life – such as *bread* or *hats* – are basically all variations of the same theme. Consider *glass* for a moment.

Glass is one of those things that we regularly come across in our daily lives: we look out of windows made of glass, we drink from a glass, and many people even put on their glasses every time they want to read a book or a newspaper or look at a computer screen. But although all glass is basically glass and made out of

the same thing – i.e. heated sand – consider how many ways it has been *altered* over the years to solve different kinds of problems:

→ It has been multiplied to keep people warm (*double glazing*)

→ It has been strengthened to keep people safe (*bulletproof glass*)

→ It has been compressed to help people communicate (*fibre optics*).

So next time you face one of life's problems, why not have a go at *altering* it, and like a **Genius** Venetian glass-blower, see where it takes you…

**P**ins, as we all know, tend to be sharp and the problem with that is pretty obvious. They can prick you.

Whether they are *drawing pins* or *tailors' pins* the point is (if you'll excuse the pun) they all have what could be called 'the ouch factor'.

In 1849, however, along came a **Cunningly Clever** thinker called William Hunt who – in a desperate attempt to pay off his debts – invented a new type of pin. A pin with one subtle *alteration*.

His pin came with a cover that didn't prick you! It was what we now know as the *safety pin* and ended up not only helping him to get out of debt, but also to stay out of debt, for the rest of his life. **Genius!**

## SAFETY PIN

## CUNNING ALTERATIONS FOR FIXING LIFE'S LITTLE PROBLEMS

### PROBLEM A I want to re-open this sealed envelope without ripping it.

### CUNNINGLY CLEVER SOLUTION *Alter* its temperature.

**E**veryone knows that one way of fixing this problem is to steam open the envelope by placing it over a recently boiled kettle. Another alternative, however, is to put it in your freezer instead whilst you focus on other tasks. Come back after a couple of hours and you should be able to prise open the envelope with a knife before re-sealing it. Admittedly your letter might end up smelling of fish fingers and green peas, but that's a different story...

## PROBLEM B I want to get rid of my mouth ulcer.

### CUNNINGLY CLEVER SOLUTION *Alter* the colour of the bananas you eat.

**Y**es, odd though it might sound, it's claimed that green bananas – as opposed to yellow bananas – can help you get rid of mouth ulcers.

*Altering* colour, however, can also make a difference in many other situations, too. For example, 'blue' light bulbs in the kitchen can help to quash your appetite if you're on a diet, and using a 'white' background can make it easier to see what you're doing when threading a needle.

## PROBLEM C I'm always losing socks, making it hard to pair them up.

### CUNNINGLY CLEVER SOLUTION *Alter* the volume of socks you buy.

**I**f you buy socks in bulk (i.e. all the same colour, all the same shape, and all the same design), firstly, they'll be much easier to put into pairs because they all look the same, and, secondly, if one occasionally goes missing, who gives a monkey's? You'll find a replacement in your sock drawer straight away…

# CUNNING ALTERATIONS FOR FIXING LIFE'S BIGGER CHALLENGES

## CHALLENGE D  Nobody wants to come to our event.

### CUNNINGLY CLEVER SOLUTION  *Alter* what you call it.

It's all too easy to underestimate the power of words. However, if it's success you're after, the words you use – or choose NOT to use – can often make a world of difference (as notorious jeweller Gerald Ratner knows only too well).

Suppose you're organising a local event or talk, for example, and only a few people want to come to it. Before you abandon the idea completely you might want to have a go at *altering* its title.

For example, the NHS was once laying on a 'Preventing Falls' course for the elderly in Bournemouth, but hardly anyone wanted to attend. Following discussions with psychologists, they came to realise that this might be because the phrase 'Preventing Falls' had too many negative associations attached to it. Consequently they *altered* the name (of exactly the same course) to 'Improving Posture' and the place was packed!

Similarly, 'Stress Management' seminars tend not to be warmly welcomed by alpha male executives in the City who think stress is for wimps. Call the same session 'Managing Pressure Positively', however, and suddenly it sounds eminently sensible to busy people with plenty of work to do.

And if you're still not convinced, you might want to reflect upon whether the following stars would have become quite so successful if they hadn't been smart enough to *alter* their own names…

TOM CRUISE MAPOTHER IV ⇨ TOM CRUISE

CHERILYN SARKISIAN LA PIERE ⇨ CHER

ERIK WEISS ⇨ HOUDINI

**PROBLEM E** I'm getting a paunch and I need to go on a diet.

**CUNNINGLY CLEVER SOLUTION** *Alter* the speed at which you eat.

I f you think about it, the key to losing weight virtually always comes down to *alterations* somewhere along the line.

It involves us either *altering* how many calories we consume (i.e. eating less) or *altering* how many calories we expend (i.e. moving more). More importantly, it also involves us *altering* our self-talk relating to food (for example, swapping the unhelpful word 'diet' for the more helpful term 'healthy eating plan') and *altering* the way many of us *use* food to escape unwanted feelings (i.e. 'emotional eating'). Some experts even suggest we set about *altering* the size of the plates we use – by avoiding large dinner plates altogether – but it's a bit more complex than that…

Anyway, one **Genius** technique recommended by many, including Paul McKenna, is to *alter* the *speed* at which we eat. In essence, you can eat pretty much what you want, when you want to, but you have to eat it really slowly and completely savour every single mouthful to the max.

Obvious though it might sound, this is a **Cunningly Clever Solution**. Why?

Because it's not uncommon for cuddly overeaters to 'shovel' down food without fully appreciating it (and, yes, like everyone else, I can be guilty of this too). McKenna's advice is that we *alter* this approach and 'eat consciously and enjoy every mouthful' by chewing it 'at least 20 times'. As suggestions go, it appears that many have found this useful…

 **BY THE WAY …** if you're still struggling to see the significance or value of the *alterations* technique for helping you to *alter* your life, please take another good look at the world around you.

**Cunning Alterations** is the reason why we have everything from speed-dating (*altered* speed) to Bikram or 'hot' yoga (*altered* temperature), keyhole surgery (*altered* size) to children's high chairs (*altered* height), and Scottish kilts (*altered* patterns) to the 101 Dalmatians (*altered* numbers).

It's also the reason why we have skyscrapers and bungalows, short haiku poems and Dostoyevsky's *War and Peace*, and warm ski-boots and cool flip-flops.

It's even the reason why the modern loo is the way it is, because **Genius** plumbers like Alexander Cumming (in 1775) and Thomas Crapper (in 1880) *altered* the shape of the piping flowing in and out of them, with their 'S-bend Stink Traps' and 'U-bends'. Probably best, however, if we skip the detail before it lowers (i.e. *alters*) the tone.

## AND FINALLY

Next time you feel in need of new ideas, here are 3 **Cunning Alterations** questions you might want to ask yourself to help you make progress:

❶ What if I could *alter* the size of what I'm doing by making it much bigger or much smaller?

❷ What if I could *alter* the speed of what I'm doing by making it much faster or much slower?

❸ What if I could *alter* my approach by tweaking the style, or shape, or structure of what I'm doing so it's much simpler and easier to use?

## THINKSPIRATION
**'Human beings can alter their lives by altering their attitudes of mind.'**
William James

**A** third highly effective way for coming up with innovative solutions for day-to-day problems is to take your mind on a 'voyage of discovery'. Or, to put it another way, to imagine you're like the captain of a ship who loves to *navigate* off into uncharted waters and explore other worlds.

It could be back in time to the world of the Romans or Vikings, or forward in time to the world of *Star Trek*. It could be across the ocean to another country (like Peru), or into the professional life of a Californian plastic surgeon or London taxi driver. To be honest, it doesn't really matter where your *navigations* take you as long as they take you somewhere else, so you can take a good look in the metaphorical mirror and ask yourself, 'What might *they* potentially do to fix it?'

Now you might be tempted into thinking this **Genius Mindtool** is absolutely bizarre, but it doesn't have to be. All it means is that you deliberately jump from one context to another. Let's go back to the Viking analogy for a second.

Supposing one of the problems you currently face is a lack of confidence when speaking in public. By stepping into an alternative world – like the world of the Vikings – you might find that you can re-frame this problem in a new and inspirational way. For example:

➔ What if you could be as brave as an axe-wielding Viking and smash your fear to smithereens?

➔ What if you could manage your anxiety by learning to meditate and visualise the calm unrippled surface of a Norwegian fjord?

➔ What if, like a longboat being rowed across the North Sea, you could go 'backwards and forwards' over your speech again and again, until you build up a 'thicker skin' allowing those irritating performance 'blisters' to eventually disappear?

➔ What if you could enrol on a public-speaking course to ensure your speech 'sizzles' like Danish Bacon?

In other words, by deliberately going off on a tangent to consider how the Vikings might be able to help you speak more confidently in public, once again you are inviting your mind to unlock its genius and consider extra angles, rather than always relying on the conventionally logical ones.

Besides, when it comes to solving day-to-day problems, there are always *linkages* between seemingly unrelated things, if we look a little deeper. For example, if it wasn't for the Vikings there'd be no such thing as 'Thursday' (named after the Viking god Thor) or 'Friday' (named after the Viking god Freya). And from a *navigation* perspective, there'd be no such thing as a 'ship' or a 'skipper' or even 'starboard', which was the large oar the Vikings placed on the right side of their boats to 'steer' them more effectively…

## CUNNING NAVIGATIONS DOODLE...

WET LEAVES ⇨ PRINGLES

THIGH BONE ⇨ EIFFEL TOWER

CRANE ⇨ KUNG FU

## CUNNING NAVIGATIONS
## NUGGET

**I**f you're into gardening – some are, some aren't – consider how one **Genius** *navigator* helped to transform the gardening world.

In 1830 a man called Edwin Budding (who worked in a textile mill in Stroud) had a **Genius Moment**. He wondered what might happen if he took the technology of an industrial mill's 'cutting velvet machine' to trim green grass instead. In other words, he made a *navigation* from the land of velvet to the land of grass! Consequently, he invented the first ever lawn mower, and made life a lot easier for gardeners than it had been for

**LAWN MOWER**

the poor medieval peasants who used to use scythes instead.

## CUNNING NAVIGATIONS
## TURNING THEORY INTO PRACTICE

Now you know what **Cunning Navigations** is all about, in a moment or two we'll be looking at how to apply it to potential challenges in your life.

WHAT A LOAD OF OLD NONSENSE!

Before that happens, however, it's really important to be upfront with you about the limitations of this particular technique.

Firstly, surprise surprise, it doesn't always work.

One person might look into a log-burning fire and simply see a log-burning fire. Another, however, might look into a log-burning fire and suddenly have a **Genius Moment**, like Thomas Smith in the 1840s who, after hearing the logs crackle, went on to invent the Christmas cracker!

Secondly, **Cunning Navigations** is not everyone's cup of tea.

In fact, cynics of creative thinking often hate this technique more than any other…

Why?

Well, without going into too much detail, *cynics love certainty*.

They feel far more comfortable knowing that the dot is safely in the middle of the square, than not knowing which of the many squares the dot is in.

Likewise, they feel far more comfortable knowing precisely what is coming up next, rather than 'not knowing' precisely what is coming up next.

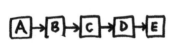 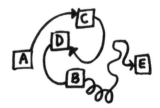

In other words, if they have a choice between the concrete and the abstract, or the sequential and the random, they'll tend to choose the concrete and the sequential every time.

Now, in many walks of life a concrete sequential mindset (as Gregorc and Butler call it) is perfectly understandable. After all, who would want to be operated on by a surgeon who says 'Ooh, I'm not entirely sure how to do this, but let's give it a go and see where it takes us'?

But if it's **Genius Moments** you're after, that's a different story.

That's when a little more of the 'abstract' and the 'random' can be very helpful. More importantly, it's when too much of the 'concrete' and too much of the 'sequential' can be distinctly unhelpful, rather like driving a car with the handbrake still on.

So please hold this thought as you continue to read about **Cunning Navigations**. With **Cunning Navigations** you can't always 'see the point of it', or 'see where it's going' at the time you're doing it. That's why it can help you to see something different...

---

## 'Talent hits a target no one else can hit; genius hits a target no one else can see.'
Arthur Schopenhauer

---

## CUNNING NAVIGATIONS FOR FIXING LIFE'S LITTLE PROBLEMS

**PROBLEM A** How can I get rid of this sticker on my window?

**CUNNINGLY CLEVER SOLUTION** *Navigate* off to your kitchen cupboard

Kitchen cupboards are often brimming with potential solutions to both tricky (and sticky) problems. Take mayonnaise, for example (which you might actually keep in the fridge, but let's not split hairs). Mayonnaise is not only good on salads it's also pretty useful if you want to get a sticker off your window, too, especially if you don't want to scratch the glass!

Or how about tomato ketchup which is sometimes used to help old copper pots gleam.

Or how about the vinegar you might have stashed on some shelf in your kitchen cupboard (which is useful if you've been stung by a wasp and are fortunately not allergic to wasp stings)? Even Hannibal, in Roman times, used vinegar to help him remove giant boulders blocking his elephant-march across the snowy Alps. Firstly, he'd have his soldiers surround the boulders with wood. Secondly, he'd get them to set fire to the wood. Thirdly, he'd get them to pour vinegar onto the hot rock so it would begin to crumble. Finally, they'd smash the rocks and march on their way...

**PROBLEM B** My biscuits have accidentally got stuck to the baking tray.

**CUNNINGLY CLEVER SOLUTION** *Navigate* off to different rooms around your house.

B elieve it or not, if you go off around your house looking for 'something' you might be able to slip between your biscuits and your baking tray (that's even thinner than a knife) you might well come across all kinds of quirky solutions.

For example, how about the dental floss you normally keep in your bathroom to give you that winning smile? Dental floss can be incredibly useful for prising things apart that have unfortunately ended up getting stuck together, from biscuits to photographs. Simply tear off a strip and gently manoeuvre it in between.

And while you're at it, perhaps take a mental note of the toothpaste you spot on the bathroom basin, too. It is said, for example, that a little Colgate toothpaste can not only help to clean silver but also the ivories of old pianos, too.

**PROBLEM C** The steps outside my house are slippery and dangerous because of the recent heavy snow, but I have no sand or salt to scatter over them.

**CUNNINGLY CLEVER SOLUTION** *Navigate* off to the world of gritty alternatives.

If you're faced with a snow problem – and you have no sand or salt at hand – you might find it helpful to let your mind wander and think about anything and everything that's 'like' sand, or 'similar' to sand such as... *cat litter*!

Yes, this solution might sound purrfectly odd, but you'd be surpised.

In January 2010 England was experiencing unusually cold weather and, as 'salt' and 'sand' supplies started to dry up (owing to excessive demand), many people did actually become highly creative and use cat litter instead. In fact, at some supermarkets in western England sales rose by 55 per cent! Admittedly, using cat litter may not have been the cheapest option (how else would it have made its inventor Ed Lowe a multi-millionaire?). However, when it came to getting rid of unwanted snow, it was a stroke of genius nonetheless.

**CHALLENGE D** I know I'm underpaid but my boss won't give me a pay rise.

**CUNNINGLY CLEVER SOLUTION** *Navigate* off to the world of TV and film.

Asking for a pay rise is notoriously difficult, even for the select few who are mega-assertive. But by allowing your mind to *navigate* off to a completely unrelated world (such as the world of TV and film) you might well be able to view the same situation from a completely different angle.

For example, suppose you end up watching an episode of *Friends*. On the one hand, all that might happen is you have a good laugh. On the other, however, you might start wondering why the main six stars ended up being paid $1.3 million each per episode. And the answer to that's simple. Because they could. By that point they had effectively become 'irreplaceable' and the TV shows couldn't be made without them.

So, with this in mind, you might start focusing on what makes *you* so unique and special, and instead of wondering, 'How can I get paid more?' start asking yourself, 'How can I be worth more?' After all, at the end of the day – as the American Motivational guru Jim Rohn used to say – we 'get paid for bringing value to the marketplace' which is why 'you need to work harder on yourself than you do at your job'.

Alternatively, you might watch the movie *Scrooge* (who gave Bob Cratchit a pay rise on Christmas Day because he was scared to death by the ghosts who visited him the night before) and focus on why your boss might be 'scared' of losing you.

Once again, it's not the TV show or film itself that matters. What matters is that, by stepping into other worlds, it can help you to contemplate other ideas.

Suppose you watch an old Charlie Chaplin silent movie, for example. This might trigger the thought of you asking for a pay rise 'silently' by getting someone else to influence your boss on your behalf. Or suppose you watch the 1969 classic *The Italian Job* (starring Michael Caine). This doesn't mean you're going to commit a robbery, or zoom around Rome in a bright red Mini. It might, however, prompt you to hatch a cunning 'plan' for getting a pay rise, instead of leaving it solely to chance...

## CUNNING NAVIGATIONS FOR FIXING LIFE'S BIGGER PROBLEMS

### CHALLENGE E I want to strike a better work–life balance.

### CUNNINGLY CLEVER SOLUTION *Navigate* your life like the captain of a ship.

It's a sad reality, but in our 24/7 world the boundaries between work and life have become amazingly blurred. No wonder many of us feel tired all the time attempting to *juggle* the day job with seeing our friends, spending quality time with our family, and perhaps even finding 'sacred time' for ourselves. So how might **Cunning Navigations** potentially help?

Well, there does appear to be some evidence to suggest that the *metaphors* we use in life can shape both our thinking and our behaviour. For example, if someone says, 'How are you?' and you groan, 'Battling on', there's a good chance your life will continually

feel like a battle; or if you repeatedly see yourself as a 'hamster on a treadmill' how can you ever expect to get off? This is why branches of psychology like NLP (Neuro Linguistic Programming) and TA (Transactional Analysis) suggest we choose our 'global metaphors' wisely if we ultimately want to achieve the results we desire.

Let's skip back to the 'captain of a ship' metaphor I mentioned earlier to illustrate the point. If you start to view yourself as the captain of your *own* ship – rather than press-ganged into serving on someone else's – there's a good chance your personal work–life balance will improve instantly because you'll be reclaiming some control. For instance:

➔ You might accept that, although 'you can't always control the wind, you can adjust the sails'

➔ You might acknowledge that even the strongest ships often need to return to harbour for important repairs and renovation to stay afloat

➔ You might even come to appreciate how work is not the be-all-and-end-all of existence and see that 'the breaking of a wave cannot explain the whole sea' (*Vladimir Nabokov*).

Alternatively, here's a **Cunning Navigations** thought for you. Sometimes, spending time out relaxing can lead to better business results than actually being at work! When Martin Cooper was watching Captain Kirk of the Starship Enterprise on TV in the early 1970s, for example, he was so inspired by the flip-up phones of the future that he went on to invent the mobile phone.

It might also be worth noting what incredible **Genius** *navigators* our early ancestors were too, always making good use of whatever they could lay their hands on. For example, in Neolithic times the antlers of deer were used as picks down in the mines, and the shoulder blades of cows were sometimes even used as shovels.

**BY THE WAY ...** strange though the **Cunning Navigations** technique might seem, once again, wherever you *navigate* off to you're likely to find evidence of it in action. For example, how many of us use the @ symbol on a daily basis when we're sending e-mails to one another? Well, originally, '@' was never intended to be used for the internet. It was an accounting symbol from the latin *ad* 'to' until **Genius** *navigator* Ray Tomlinson became the first person to use it in this novel way in 1972.

So next time you need some fresh ideas, why not make good use of your 'travelling mind' (as Robert Louis Stevenson used to call it). Either allow your mind to travel to *interesting places* to bring wonderful ideas back – like Marco Polo returning from China to

Italy with pasta, or the crusaders returning from the Holy Land with the clever Saracens' cedar-wood solution for getting rid of moths – or perhaps do it the other way around: *navigate* off with whatever you have to apply it in *unusual* or *unexpected places*. I recently read, for example, that *salt* is used by people in over 14,000 different ways, from preserving food to the manufacturing of industrial detergents. Or what about Theodore Maiman. 'Theodore who?' you're probably wondering. Back in 1960 Theodore Maiman invented the *laser* and didn't know what to do with it! It took him about four years to realise it might be useful for improving eyesight. Anyway, thanks to **Cunning Navigations** it's now used in over 101 different ways, from precision engineering to healing patients undergoing medical surgery.

## AND FINALLY

Here are 3 questions for stimulating **Cunning Navigations** which you might want to ask yourself next time you're getting nowhere:

❶ What if I could temporarily leave my problem behind and *navigate* off into a parallel world for fresh ideas?

❷ What else *out there* could potentially help me to fix this challenge?

❸ How might the 'asp-irational' Cleopatra have got around this particular problem, or the three Musketeers, or the super-sleuth Hercule Poirot?

## THINKSPIRATION
'A ship in harbour is safe, but that is not what ships are for.'
John A. Shedd

**A** fourth CUNNING CAN**DO** technique for coming up with **Cunningly Clever Solutions** for solving day-to-day problems is to ask yourself what might happen if you suddenly switched, swapped, or changed *direction*.

After all, this approach is the reason we have everything from upside-down cake to movie prequels, and indoor fireworks to stressed out City-types wanting to downsize. It's also how J.K. Rowling reversed the word warthogs to create Hogwarts.

So next time you sit down to watch a film like *The Curious Case of Benjamin Button* (in which a man born old gets progressively younger), or *Monsters Inc* (in which monsters are scared of children instead of children being afraid of monsters), or perhaps even listen to a song like Lilly Allen's 'It's not me, it's you' (when the familiar cliché is 'It's not you, it's me') bear in mind that **Cunning Directions** is a highly versatile tool.

It's also important to note, however, that changing *direction* does not always have to require you changing your *physical direction*, such as walking through a doorway backwards to help carry a heavy new sofa into your sitting room: it can also be applied to spinning your *psychological direction* around too!

For example, what might happen if you started to focus on problem avoidance rather than problem solving, such as proactively going to your dentist for regular check-ups instead of delaying the inevitable and ending up with painful and expensive root canal treatment instead?

Or, what if you're faced with the unfortunate problem of a relationship breakdown in which your partner has walked out on you? As Anthony Robbins – the American peak-performance guru – suggests, instead of depressing yourself by thinking, 'I wasn't good enough so they left me', how about you spin this negative into a positive by thinking, 'Thank God they left, so they left room in my life for someone who's right for me'?

## CUNNING DIRECTIONS DOODLE...

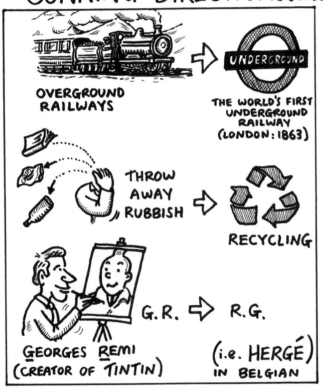

OVERGROUND RAILWAYS ⇒ THE WORLD'S FIRST UNDERGROUND RAILWAY (LONDON: 1863)

THROW AWAY RUBBISH ⇨ RECYCLING

GEORGES REMI (CREATOR OF TINTIN) G.R. ⇨ R.G. (i.e. HERGÉ) IN BELGIAN

Jürgen Klinsmann was one of the best football players of his day, scoring many goals for both club and country. Klinsmann, however, was famous not only for his talent. The West German football ace also had a dreadful reputation for 'diving' on the pitch in order to win penalties or free kicks. So when he moved to Tottenham Hotspur in 1994, many football fans gave him a frosty reception, especially because some felt his 'diving' behaviour had helped knock England out of the World Cup.

Klinsmann, however, used **Cunning Directions** to win them over. The moment he scored his first goal for his new side against Sheffield Wednesday, he celebrated by doing a funny dive which the crowd loved.

From then on, he and his teammates would instantly dive every time he scored a goal in a match, and it became his personal trademark. **Genius!**

## CUNNING DIRECTIONS FOR FIXING
## LIFE'S LITTLE PROBLEMS

**CHALLENGE A** I'm really bored.

**CUNNINGLY CLEVER SOLUTION** Switch *direction* and start seeing boredom in a positive rather than negative light.

None of us likes being bored if we can possibly help it, especially if we have a 'low boredom threshold'. Please bear in mind, however, that there's always an upside to a downside

and boredom is no exception. To a genius, for example, boredom often means fantastic 'ideas time', 'thinking time', 'planning time' and 'creative time'.

For example, in 1979 Canadians Chris Haney and Scott Abbott were bored playing Scrabble over and over again so they ended up inventing their own boardgame instead. They went on to call it Trivial Pursuit and it turned them both into multi-millionaires!

Likewise, Sir Arthur Conan Doyle used to get incredibly 'bored' as a 27-year-old doctor in a small surgery with very few patients to attend to, so, to keep his mind occupied, he started writing Sherlock Holmes novels instead.

So next time you feel bored, why not use your 'gift of time' to come up with something truly magical? Besides, it's no coincidence that Michelangelo once said **'Genius is eternal patience...'**

## CHALLENGE B  I can't get the medicine to go down.

### CUNNINGLY CLEVER SOLUTION  Switch *direction* (and no, I don't mean that)

Mary Poppins may well have been spot-on when she said, 'A spoonful of sugar makes the medicine go down'. However, this isn't the only way to fix the problem.

If the medicine you have to take, for example, is really 'yucky', then waiting for a lump of sugar afterwards might be too long to wait. If so, switch *direction* and take action *before* you take the medicine as well as after it. Some experts, for example, suggest you use an ice cube to numb your tongue first; that way the taste is unlikely to bother you too much.

Alternatively, if you're trying to help your young child swallow a pill (which is surprisingly tricky for many kids), suggest they switch *direction* and put their pill *under* their tongue rather than on top of it. This way it's far less likely to pop out of their mouth every other second...

**CHALLENGE C**  The barrier of the car park exit is jammed.

**CUNNINGLY CLEVER SOLUTION**  Switch *direction* and drive out of the entrance.

This is an example Edward de Bono gives of someone who was once genuinely stuck in a car park. They then asked themselves, 'What would Edward de Bono do in this situation?' – and came up with this lateral solution.

Obviously, I'm not suggesting you make a habit of driving out of entrances or driving into exits (unless you're a Hollywood stunt-driver), but the point being made is an important one. If the usual way ahead is blocked, switch *direction* and find an unusual way out...

**CHALLENGE D** Whenever I'm giving a talk, people in the audience switch off the moment I read out information from my hand-held notes.

**CUNNINGLY CLEVER SOLUTION** Switch the *direction* of your eyes.

Leaving PowerPoint and Autocue aside for now, when the majority of speakers read out information from hand-held notes during a talk they usually do the following with their eyes. They look *down – up – down*. *Down* at what they're going to say, *up* at their audience to check if they're still there, and then finally – having lost their train of thought – *down* at their notes again. A bit like this…

Experts on presentation skills, however, suggest we reverse this process and look *up–down–up* instead. The reason's very simple. Audiences tend to listen most at the beginning, and at the end, but 'wander off' in the middle. So, with the first option, all the audience is likely to see is a man talking to a piece of paper. Consequently, they feel disconnected and switch off! With the second option, however, what the audience sees is a speaker who not only makes a lot of eye contact with them throughout, but also appears to know their speech off by heart (because they're looking at the ceiling or out of the window when the speaker's actually looking down at their notes).

**PROBLEM E** Supposing a stranger grabs me by the wrist. How can I break free?

**CUNNINGLY CLEVER SOLUTION** Change the *direction* in which your pull your hand.

Most people – who have no self-defence training – instinctively pull away if someone grabs their wrist. After all, why wouldn't they? It makes perfect sense. If someone wants you to go one way, and you want to go the other, you *pull*. Perfectly logical.

Nope.

The trouble with this approach is that, unless you're a lot stronger than your attacker, you're inadvertently giving them the advantage. This is because when you pull your wrist away in a straight line there's a good chance you're driving your wrist directly into the *strongest* part of their grip (i.e. where their four fingers are locked together).

Far better to change *direction* and go the other way and *push* through the weakest part of their grip (i.e. where their poor little thumb is on its own). Simply twist up and away you go.

**BY THE WAY ...** be prepared to accept that **Cunning Directions** can often take you in all kinds of strange *directions*. For example, it might help you to become a little more 'experimental' in what you choose to wear and how you choose to wear it, although fashion is clearly a personal thing...

UNDERPANTS

OVERPANTS

Alternatively, **Cunning Directions** can be used to help you combat many of the toughest 'battles' or challenges you might be facing in your personal life. For example, it could inspire you to *turn your thinking around* so you finally face up to your fears rather than run away from them, or perhaps you tell someone how much you love them *before* it's too late.

And if you think this 'battle-winning' claim sounds a bit far-fetched, please think again… A number of real battles throughout history have been won precisely because of the **Cunning Directions** technique!

For example, Admiral Nelson won the Battle of Aboukir Bay in 1798 by sailing ridiculously close to the shoreline in Egypt and going *behind* Napoleon's ships whose heavy cannons were all pointing the other way (i.e. out to sea). By the time the French navy had turned their guns around, they'd already lost the battle.

Similarly, **Cunning Directions** is the reason why Bonnie Prince Charlie was out-smarted at the Battle of Culloden in 1745. Up until then the 'Highland Charge' – as it was called – had worked perfectly well. Wild Scottish Highlanders used to run down a hill screaming and yelling to scare the living daylights out of the enemy. Then they'd push their enemy's muskets out of the way with the shields on their left arm, and slash them with the broadswords held in their right. At Culloden, however, the Duke of Cumberland had trained his Hanoverian soldiers to prepare for this tactic. As a result, Cumberland's soldiers were told to aim their musket – not at the man directly in front of them

– but at the man to the *side* of the man in front. In other words, at their buddy's opponent rather than their own. Consequently, when the Jacobites did their 'predictable' attack, they left their torsos completely exposed to enemy muskets coming from an 'unexpected' angle!

But maybe these examples are a bit too heavy; here are a few lighter ones to cheer ourselves up a bit.

Prior to the 1968 Olympics in Mexico, high-jumpers had always jumped forwards because that's the way high-jumpers had always jumped. But then along came a man called Fosbury who decided to jump backwards instead. Not only did he win the Gold Medal but also the 'Fosbury flop' made him famous, and his superior technique has been used ever since.

Or – keeping the mood light – where would TV quiz shows be if it wasn't for **Cunning Directions**? There'd be no Anne Robinson's *The Weakest Link* (which turned being nasty from a minus into a plus) and no Stephen Fry's *QI* (a **Genius** show that has managed to turn IQ into popular entertainment).

Come to think of it, there'd probably be no superstars like Madonna either, who has switched *direction* numerous times throughout her career, helping to keep her music fresh and relevant in a highly competitive industry.

So there you have it. As with the other techniques you'll find evidence of **Cunning Directions** wherever you look, from reflector sunglasses to reverse psychology, endoscopes to anatomist Gunther Von Hagens's rather odd 'Inside-Out' exhibitions, and even preventative medicine such as Vicks First Defence which claims to 'stop your cold before it takes hold'.

# AND FINALLY

Next time you feel 'stuck', here are 3 **Cunning Directions** questions you might want to ask yourself to help you find a different way:

**❶** What if I potentially changed *direction* and turned this problem inside out, or upside down, or back to front?

**❷** What if I potentially changed the order and sequence in which I did things, so the end became the beginning and the beginning became the end?

**❸** What if I could spin this problem around and see it as a potential opportunity instead?

---

## THINKSPIRATION

## 'If you do not change direction there is a good chance you will end up where you are heading.'

Lao Tzu

---

**F**inally, the fifth dynamic way for coming up with **Cunningly Clever** ideas for fixing life's problems is to identify what you would *normally* do in a specific situation, and then imagine yourself doing the complete opposite!

So if, for example, you want to write a best-selling book and don't know what to call it, consider how author Toby Young took a well-known title like *How to Win Friends and Influence People* and turned it into *How to Lose Friends and Alienate People*. Or consider how J.M. Barrie opposed the idea that all boys need to grow up and ended up creating Peter Pan. Or if you're fussing and fretting about where to go for your next 'vacation', ask yourself what might happen if you deliberately opposed this idea and didn't go anywhere at all, opting for a 'staycation' instead.

What's great about this technique is that it gives you the complete freedom to think the unthinkable, and radically challenge 'the rules'. And just in case you are not entirely convinced by how effective the **Cunning Oppositions** technique can be, here's a little food for thought.

Historically, superheroes – like Superman, Wonder Woman and Captain America – were predictably young, fit and athletic. In 2004, however, the animation company Pixar *opposed* these rules, and introduced a middle-aged, out-of-shape superhero by the name of *Mr Incredible,* earning them millions of dollars in the process.

So please don't be afraid to *oppose* your own life's rules from time to time. If it wasn't for *oppositions* there'd be no anti-heroes like Captain Jack Sparrow in *The Pirates of the Caribbean* or Asterix & Obelix, no Banksy murals, no seven-minute long 'Bohemian Rhapsody' and, come to think of it, no Beatles (who 'wrote their own songs' and even featured an Indian sitar on the song 'Norwegian Wood' back in 1968). But please don't think that being *oppositional* only applies to the world of sex, drugs and rock-n-roll. Quite the opposite!

Consider how Florence Nightingale *opposed* the 'rules' of nursing in the Crimean War to develop a more humane way of treating

injured soldiers; consider how Elizabeth Fry *opposed* the 'rules' of prison conditions in the Victorian era to create a more humane way of treating prisoners; and consider how Gandhi *opposed* the 'rules' of political resistance, by showing how much could be achieved through 'non-violence'. Or what about the **Genius** designer James Dyson who has endlessly *opposed* design 'rules' – from air-dryers to vacuum cleaners – and revolutionised six industries!

## CUNNING OPPOSITIONS DOODLE...

## CUNNING OPPOSITIONS NUGGET

**H**ow many of us check our wristwatch every day to tell the time?

Well, it wasn't always this way. In the nineteenth century, those wealthy enough to own Mad Hatter-type pocket watches kept them in their waistcoat pockets, attached by a metal chain.

In 1904, however, along came the **Genius** *oppositional thinker* Louise Cartier who deliberately broke this rule by coming up with the idea of a 'wristwatch' instead. Yes, it might seem pretty obvious now, but back then it was… well, quite the opposite.

## CUNNING OPPOSITIONS FOR FIXING LIFE'S LITTLE PROBLEMS

**PROBLEM A** My young child's finding it hard to remember their 9 times table…

**CUNNINGLY CLEVER SOLUTION** *Oppose* the idea that children always need to work out numbers in their head and suggest they work them out on their hands instead.

**F**orgive me if you happen to know this trick already, but when it comes to remembering your 9 times table (and unfortunately it only works with 9), whatever number you are multiplying 9 by

ask your child to fold down that finger on their two outstretched hands. So if it's 9 × 4, for example, ask them to fold down their 'fourth' finger, or if it's 9 × 7 ask them to fold down their 'seventh' finger.

What they'll find is that 'the answer' is right in front of them! All they need do is count the fingers to the left of the folded finger, and then those to the right (and don't worry too much about whether a thumb officially counts as a finger… in this exercise fingers and thumbs are all the same).

FOLD DOWN 4ᵗʰ FINGER

$$9 \times 4 = 36$$

FOLD DOWN 7ᵗʰ FINGER

So if it's their seventh finger that your child has folded down, they'll instantly see that 9 × 7 is 6… 3! Hopefully this top tip – by **Genius** maths teacher Rob

$$9 \times 7 = 63$$

Eastaway – can help your child to realise that there are often simple solutions to complex problems if we approach them in **Cunningly Clever** ways…

## PROBLEM B I've accidentally spilled red wine on the white carpet.

**CUNNINGLY CLEVER SOLUTION** *Oppose* the idea of cleaning it up straight away and pour some white wine on it first.

Although this might sound counterintuitive (i.e. pouring on more wine when all you want to do is clean up the wine you've already spilled), adding white wine can help to dilute the redness, and not only make it easier to clean up but also less likely to stain.

While you're at it, however, you might also want to reflect upon what an amazingly counterintuitive world we live in. For example, ever noticed how 'opposites attract' when it comes to love? Or why we don't always know what we've got until it's gone? Or how, if you're talking to people at a social event, sometimes 'the less wine there is in the bottle, the more noise it makes when it's poured out'?

Finally, here's one more 'counterintuitive' insight to mull over.

When Radio One DJ Mike Read refused to play the Frankie Goes to Hollywood pop song 'Relax' back in 1984 on moral grounds, and the BBC followed suit and banned it, their actions ended up accidentally having the opposite effect than the one they'd hoped for. The ban on the controversial song created such a buzz of publicity that the single ended up going straight to Number One within two weeks, and then ended up staying there for another four! Had they done the 'opposite' (and got incredibly dated and uncool DJs to say how much they loved it) it might never have been such a monster *smash*…

## PROBLEM C  I'm getting nowhere talking to this idiot.

## CUNNINGLY CLEVER SOLUTION  *Oppose* the idea that you're talking to an idiot.

**M**any years ago I was given a piece of invaluable advice: 'If you think you're talking to an idiot so do they!'

So with this in mind, next time you feel like you're talking to a complete and utter fool, you might find it helpful to *oppose* this idea, especially if you want to reach a successful outcome.

Firstly, do your best to separate the person from the behaviour. Yes, they might have done something foolish, but that doesn't necessarily make them a fool. All people have unconditional worth, value and dignity as human beings, it's just with some you have to dig a little deeper to find it.

Secondly, you might even want to stop 'talking to' them and start 'talking with' them. It's a subtle difference, but it means that your conversation will instantly become less parent–child and combative.

Finally, you might want to take note of Richard Carlson's view on the matter; the author who wrote the best-seller *Don't Sweat the Small Stuff* (yet another example of **Cunning Oppositions** in action!). Carlson suggests that it can be helpful sometimes to 'imagine that everyone is enlightened except for    you'. Carlson admits that it's far from easy to do this. However, he champions the view that at some level we can potentially 'learn' something from everyone we meet... OM...

## CUNNING OPPOSITIONS FOR FIXING LIFE'S BIGGER CHALLENGES

**CHALLENGE D** I keep sending out my CV to try and get a job but I'm getting absolutely nowhere.

**CUNNINGLY CLEVER SOLUTION** *Oppose* the idea of sending out your CV and become your CV instead.

If you're struggling to get work, you might want to explore what the University of Kent's Career Service calls *Creative Job Hunting*, which is based on the idea that the majority of jobs are *not* advertised. Simply get out there and get noticed, because at the end of the day 'Life's a pitch!'

For example, a history graduate called David Rowe got a job by walking down Fleet Street in London 'wearing sandwich boards asking for a month's work experience'. He got a placement from an 'international recruitment firm' almost straight away who were impressed with him taking the initiative. Clearly, if everyone did the same thing, the 'novelty factor' would be lost. But the point is that not everyone does, or would dare to...

Alternatively, here's another **Cunning Opposition** for you. When my dad sadly lost his job in advertising back in the 1970s – because the company was asset-stripped – he came to realise it was much easier to sell others than to sell himself. So he set up his own recruitment company in advertising finding other people jobs instead. Ironically, a few years down the line, a few of his senior bosses who had pushed him and others out of their jobs came to him asking for help finding them a new job! And lastly, why not think about *opposing* the 'rules' of CVs to make yours stand out from the crowd? For example, send a jigsaw CV or a musical CV (depending on who it's for, obviously)…

### PROBLEM E  I keep searching for happiness but I still can't find it.

**CUNNINGLY CLEVER SOLUTION**  *Oppose* the idea of searching for happiness because – as they say in Zen – 'When you seek it, you cannot find it.'

**K**riss Akabusi – the former Olympic hurdler – once shared the following 'Cat's Tail' story with me, which seems to sum up *oppositional* thinking pretty well.

> **There was once a cat who thought that happiness was in its tail.**
>
> **So it chased it and chased it, ever faster and ever faster.**
>
> **Unable to catch it, it kept getting more and more tired until it finally collapsed with exhaustion.**
>
> **Eventually, after resting for some time, it got up and went on its way.**
>
> **What happened? Happiness simply followed it wherever it went…**

JCB?

**BY THE WAY...** as with all the other CUNNING CAN**DO** techniques in this book you'll find that **Cunning Oppositions** is a lot more widespread than it might appear.

For example, next time you go shopping take a good look around you.

If you're at your local pharmacy you might notice that brands like NIVEA (which traditionally only provided creams and beauty products for women) now provide a range of deodorants and creams for men, too.

Or if you're in a pub or a restaurant you might notice that Stella Artois (which has been producing Belgian beer since the thirteenth century) now produces cider – or what it calls cidre – as well.

Or next time you're getting cash out of the local ATM, bear in mind that cashpoint machines only exist because the old rules of banking were once *opposed*. Historically, you had to go into a bank to get your money out, and you also needed the help of a cashier. In 1967, however, at Barclays Bank in Enfield, London, John Shepherd-Barron invented and installed the first ever ATM which meant you didn't have to go into the bank to get your money out, and you didn't need the help of a cashier either.

And so it goes on. Most people, for example, are brought up by 'human' parents of one kind or another. In 1914, however, U.S. author Edgar Rice Burroughs *opposed* this concept and wrote a story of a boy – orphaned in the jungle – who was brought up by apes instead, and he named him Tarzan.

## AND FINALLY

Here are 2 questions for stimulating **Cunning Oppositions** which you might want to ask yourself next time you feel your personal potential is being stifled (and yes, I'm deliberately including only 2 questions because I'm *opposing* my own rule of 3 questions per technique!)

❶ What if I *oppose* the way I normally do this, and do it an intriguingly different way instead?

❷ What if I write down all the rules for this situation and then imagine myself breaking them one by one?

## THINKSPIRATION
### 'Whatever you think, think the opposite.'
Paul Arden

# THE DECEPTIVE POWER OF A 'TWIST OF THOUGHT'

**'Our life is what our thoughts make of it.'**

Marcus Aurelius

**U**p until now, we've looked at how CUNNING CAN**DO** can help you to fix all kinds of challenges in your life.

What if, however, you happen to be one of those amazing people whose sights are set higher than a better job, mending the kitchen cupboard and finding a new date? What if you genuinely have aspirations to *change the world and make it a better place*?

Well, the good news is that you can apply the same 5 principles you've just learnt about to much bigger problems too: **Global Problems** such as social problems, political problems and environmental problems.

And with this in mind I hope the following examples will inspire you to come up with **Global Genius Solutions** of your own...

## Country:  Brazil
## Issue:  Poverty and litter

In 1988 an architect called Jaime Lerner became the newly appointed Mayor of the city of Curitiba in Brazil. The city had many problems that needed fixing, but two in particular: poor nutrition amongst the local population who could not afford healthy food, and lots of litter on the streets, which was not only unsightly but also a health hazard.

So what did he do? He used his **Cunningly Clever** mind to ask the question, 'What if we *connected* these two problems together?' As a result, he devised a scheme in which for every two bags of rubbish people collected and brought in they would be given one box of free food.

As a result, the streets became instantly cleaner, and the poorest in the community began to receive a much better diet. **Genius!**

**Country:** Australia

**Issue:** Anti-social behaviour

In 2006 local officials in Sydney, Australia, didn't know what to do with disruptive youths who kept hanging out in a car park in Rockdale, revving their car engines and booming out loud music. The place was seen as a 'cool' place to go, and it was difficult to change this perception. So what did they do? They used their **Cunningly Clever** minds to ask the question, 'What if we could alter the sound of the car park in some way?' As a result, they began to broadcast Barry Manilow's 'Copacabana' at high volume.

In doing so, the car park instantly became uncool, and the youths decided to flee, as did several of the local residents. By the way, no disrespect intended to Barry Manilow fans; it could easily have had the opposite effect in other cities, and also 'Could it be Magic', based on the Chopin classic, was, in my humble opinion, a bit of a winner! Anyway, what the Sydney example shows is how a simple **Twist of Thought** can often help to shift behaviour. And just in case you're thinking, 'But this only displaces the problem, it doesn't fix it', good point, but we'll address the issue of '*buts*' later.

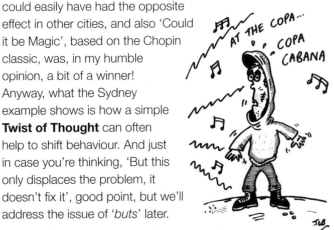

Finally, it might also be worth reflecting how, in 2009, in north Lincolnshire, UK, the local council introduced a similar idea to tackle anti-social behaviour in their underpasses, but this time ended up focusing on *altering* lighting rather than sound. Evidently, pink lighting 'shows up acne' and, for obvious reasons, no self-conscious teenager would ever want to be seen in that light…

# CUNNING NAVIGATIONS

## Country: United Kingdom
## Issue: Fighting disease

When Paul Nurse and his team of scientists set out to discover a way of controlling cancer cell growth in humans in 1974, the most logical place to focus their attention would have been looking at the human body.

Nurse, however, decided to *navigate* off to somewhere completely different; the world of *beer* (or *yeast* to be more specific).

Evidently – according to Richard Platt in his book *Eureka* – studying yeast is about 80 times less complicated than studying people (from a DNA perspective), which makes it much easier to spot what's going on in terms of 'genes' and 'cells'.

As a result of this rather unusual *navigation*, Nurse's team went on to identify the cdc2 gene in human DNA, and in 2001 Nurse was awarded a Nobel Prize for this scientific breakthrough. Thanks to their highly unusual way of thinking, doctors are now better placed to understand how cancer cells divide out of control and also how to stop them growing without harming healthy organisms.

And this is only one of numerous biomimicry *navigations* helping the world of medicine to solve problems today. For example, scientists are looking at the secrets of zebra fish to help them combat heart disease, hyenas to help them improve people's immune systems, and even salamanders to find ways of helping amputees hopefully one day re-grow their limbs.

**Country:** South Africa
**Issue:** Political reconciliation

**W**hen Nelson Mandela was finally released on 11 February 1990 after 27 years in prison, many feared that South Africa was heading for a bloody civil war.

Mandela could easily have sought revenge on the white minority who had incarcerated him during apartheid. However, he decided to help guide South Africa in a completely different *direction*... the *direction* of peace and reconciliation.

(In fact, it might be worth reflecting on how the word 'reconciliation' is basically all about shifting *direction* and means 'to bring together again'.)

As a result of this reversed approach, both Mandela and President F.W. de Klerk shared the Nobel Peace Prize in 1993.

Two years later, in 1995, Mandela then used **Cunning Directions** again. This time, he used it to help 'reverse' many South Africans' perceptions of the Springbok rugby team when he handed the Rugby World Cup to the victorious South African captain Francois Pienaar... wearing his very own Springbok shirt.

## Country: The Netherlands
## Issue: Flooding

**B**ecause of its incredible flatness, the low-lying Netherlands has always been vulnerable to flooding.

Consequently, throughout its history, all kinds of **Genius** water engineers have ended up having to use their **Cunningly Clever** minds to keep the invading sea at bay.

Increasingly, however, the Dutch are beginning to *oppose* the idea that all houses need to be built on dry land. In an article by Joe Palca, entitled 'Dutch Architects Plan for a Floating Future', we're told of how in the town of Maasbommel they've been building 'floating houses' whose foundations rest on the bottom of the river; if the river level rises because of flooding then the house and its foundations rise too, and 'flexible pipes' mean that electrical and sewage services can still be maintained.

As Chris Zevenbergen of the design company Dura Vermeer tells Palca, 'In the past, the Dutch only built homes in places where dikes made flooding unlikely. The concept that in fact you build in an area where a flood may occur is completely new.'

And it doesn't stop there. Dutch *oppositional* thinkers are now also exploring ways of floating gardens and entire cities too! Waterworld here we come...

The purpose of sharing these examples with you is simply to shed light on how *deceptively powerful* a **Twist of Thought** can be.

One only needs to look at a mosquito (the biggest killer in Africa) or a skilled martial artist striking a pressure point, for example, to realise how time and again it's often the miniscule things in life that end up having the biggest impact.

And – forgive me for getting carried away here – but I genuinely believe that ALL of the big breakthroughs in human history can be traced back to CUNNING CAN**DO** shifts in thinking, somewhere along the line. For example, consider how:

→ The Ancient Mesopotamians used **Cunning Navigations** to apply a potter's wheel to the world of transport

→ The **Genius** Galileo, like Copernicus before him, used **Cunning Directions** to argue that the Earth orbited around the Sun rather than the Sun around the Earth (although he did end up getting tortured for suggesting this, so go easy with some of your more controversial ideas!).

→ **Genius** Abraham Darby used **Cunning Connections** to combine *coke + the process of smelting iron ore* back in 1779, and in the process kick-started the Industrial Revolution.

So there you have it.

Creative thinking is not always the namby-pamby fluffy subject people take it to be. In fact, I always say creativity is rather like a swordfish... it might appear to be wet and wishy-washy, but it can also have a serious point to it!

But that's enough about swordfish.

In the next section of this book you will be introduced to a variety of **Genius Thinking Tools** for helping you to achieve greater levels of success in your professional life.

Before we move on, however, 'there's just one more thing' (as the **Genius** TV detective Lieutenant Columbo used to say).

If you genuinely want to sharpen your **Genius Thinking Skills**, it's vital you develop what Professor John Adair calls a 'wide span of reference'. If you're not entirely sure what this means, please allow me to briefly explain…

## DEVELOPING A WIDE SPAN OF REFERENCE

To someone with a *narrow* span of reference a 'frog is a frog' and a 'spaceship is a spaceship'. They belong in two totally different spheres, and have absolutely nothing in common with one another.

To someone with a *wide* span of reference, however, this 'ain't necessarily so'.

Firstly, for example, they might notice that frogs on a lily pond and aliens in Hollywood sci-fi movies really do look remarkably similar, with eyes at the side of their head and long pointy fingers…

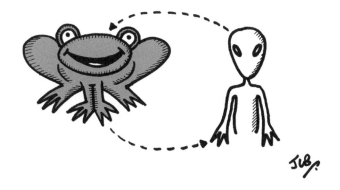

Secondly, they might notice that the shape of a frog's head and the shape of a flying saucer are pretty similar too.

Thirdly, they might even relect upon how shiny they both are, or how easy they both find it to fly through the air, or perhaps even how both frogs and flying saucers have had children's sweets named after them (e.g. sherbet Flying Saucers and Freddo chocolate frogs).

Yes, I know we're back to aliens and spaceships again, but the underlying insight is an important one. Developing a 'wide span of reference' is important because geniuses frequently spot the hidden relationships and subtle interconnections between unrelated objects, that others fail to spot.

Developing a 'wide span of reference' can be applied to *any* situation in which a touch of genius is needed.

Take the tough macho world of the Army, for example.

To someone with a *narrow* span of reference the idea that wacky 'Cubist art', or sloppy 'custard', or children's 'party-poppers' could ever be of help to serious soldiers with serious work to do, would probably never even cross their radar.

To a **Genius Thinker**, however, they might not be so separate after all…

→ **FACT:** Cubist art was used in the early 1900s to help create designs for military camouflage.

MODERNIST
ART OF
FRANZ MARC

CAMOUFLAGE
(1916)

➔ **FACT:** New body armour is now being manufactured by BAE which mirrors the way molecules of 'custard' contract upon impact (because with custard, the faster the impact, it, the faster it closes up).

LIQUID 'BULLET PROOF' ARMOUR (2010)

➔ **FACT:** Two former SAS soldiers I've had conversations with – Robin Horsfall and Andy McNab – highlighted how, in the absence of expensive U.S. equipment for detecting tripwires, SAS operatives sometimes use children's 'party-poppers instead. Why? Because, when fired, the party-poppers release thin paper threads that are light enough to prevent tripwires being activated, yet also colourful enough to see from a distance...

Finally, as we draw this section on 'The deceptive power of a Twist of Thought' to a close, please remember that **Genius Ideas** don't always need to be complicated.

More often than not, the simpler the idea, the better...

➔ Think of how the **Genius** composer John Williams's theme tune to the film *Jaws* used only two notes.

➔ Think of how the brilliant Arabic idea of the 'zero' revolutionised the world of mathematics, making it much easier for us to count in large numbers rather than use traditional Roman numerals.

→ Think of how **Cunningly Clever** Albert J. Parkhouse – who was unable to hang up his coat one day at the U.S. wire company where he worked because all the coat hooks were already taken – improvised and created the modern wire coat hanger instead.

→ Think of how the invention of the stirrup in the eighth century revolutionised Western society by making it possible for knights in heavy armour to sit on a horse without falling off.

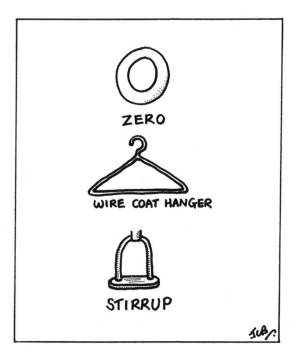

**'Nothing is more powerful than an idea whose time has come.'**

Victor Hugo

# GEN!US
# AT WORK

Cunningly Clever Creativity for
boosting business success

'To make headway, improve your
head.'

B.C. Forbes (founder of *Forbes* magazine)

# INTRODUCTION

'Imagination is more
important than knowledge.'

Albert Einstein

The purpose of this next section of the book is simple.

It is to help you come up with **Genius Ideas** whenever you might need them, in a business context.

In this respect, the same principles apply whether you are the CEO of a major corporation who is keen to build competitive advantage, or a manager who wants to bring out the best in your team. Likewise, they are equally relevant whether you are self-employed and fighting to keep your head above water, or a budding entrepreneur who's looking for that 'big idea' for making your first million.

This does not mean that it will 'guarantee' you greater business success, but what it will do is encourage you to open your mind up to a variety of alternative, and additional, solutions you may not have considered before.

In the process you'll discover 26 practical idea-generation tools for applying to your own unique professional situation.

In addition to this, you'll also find a treasure chest of examples showing how **Cunningly Clever Creativity** has been embraced by countless geniuses in the world of business to achieve truly outstanding results.

I genuinely hope you find it entertaining, thought-provoking, inspirational and, most of all… *useful*.

Before we begin, however, maybe it would be a good idea (please excuse yet another pun) to give you a whistle-stop tour of 'creativity' to help set the scene.

Here goes.

# 7 ANSWERS TO 7 QUESTIONS

## 1 WHAT IS CREATIVITY?

It's basically 'the defeat of habit by
originality' (*Arthur Koestler*) or, to put it
another way, it's 'the making of the new
and the re-arranging of the old in new
ways' (*Michael Vance*).

## 2 CAN ANYONE BE CREATIVE?

Yes, although, funnily enough, for years the answer to this
question used to be 'no'.

In the time of the Ancient Greeks, for example, creativity was seen
as a gift from the gods. If you wanted to be creative you had to be
lucky and wait patiently for your Muse to come and inspire you.

Then, many centuries later in the 1800s, the Romantic poets (like
Byron, Wordsworth and Shelley) took a different view. Creativity,
in their eyes, was not so much a gift from the gods, but more of
an innate gift. If you wanted to be creative you simply had to be
'special' – in other words rather like them and their mates and not
any old riff-raff.

Nowadays, however (largely thanks to the pioneering work of
psychologists and educationalists like J.P. Guilford, Edward de
Bono and Tony Buzan), creativity has come to be regarded as a
cognitive skill which can be 'learnt, taught and improved'. Or more
to the point, re-learnt, because we were all creative once upon a
time as young children, before we had this natural ability schooled
out of us by the double whammy of *criticism* and *conformity*.

Clearly this doesn't mean that we all have it within us to become
the next Mozart or Leonardo da Vinci. Of course not. What it does
mean is that, 'Creativity is like height and weight. We all have
different amounts, but we all have some' (*Winston Fletcher*).

## 3 WHO SAYS 'CREATIVITY IS IMPORTANT IN THE MODERN WORLD OF BUSINESS'?

Well, just about everyone really. But two of the most compelling groups are:

→ Business billionaires like Bill Gates (co-founder of Microsoft) who says it's 'the most important quality a person can possess', and Lakshmi Mittal who states, 'Always think outside the box and embrace opportunities that appear, wherever they might be.'

→ Tip-top academics writing for journals like the *Harvard Business Review* who highlight that 'ideas and innovation are the most precious currency in the new economy'.

Yup, to be honest, the list is endless. Most now agree that the modern economy is essentially a 'creative economy', where ideas have become the new scarce resource.

## 4 WHAT'S THE LINK BETWEEN CREATIVITY AND INNOVATION?

There's a long answer to this question, and a short one. Here's the short one. Innovation = applied creativity. Innovation involves taking a new 'creative' idea and then exploiting it for commercial or organisational advantage.

## 5 WHAT IS 'LATERAL THINKING'?

Lateral thinking is 'the seeking to solve problems by apparently illogical means'. Although the phrase itself was created and made famous by Edward de Bono back in the late 1960s, its origins go back much further.

Take the Trojan horse, for example. For years and years the Ancient Greeks kept trying to find a way inside the gates of Troy by using conventional, traditional and 'vertical' methods of attack. Time after time, however, they failed.

Then one day their army decided to get **Cunningly Creative** and come at the same problem from a different angle. 'What if we built a huge wooden horse, filled it with soldiers, left it outside the gates as a "gift" and waited for the Trojans to say, "Ooh, thanks very much, what a kind present", and drag it back in?'

Totally crazy? Definitely. But it worked and, at the end of the day, that's what counts. In the words of a famous Chinese proverb, 'It doesn't matter if the cat is black or white, as long as it catches the mouse.'

And this is why, with lateral thinking, so-called crazy ideas are often regarded as perfectly sensible, once they have been shown to work.

## 6 WHAT'S THE SECRET OF COMING UP WITH NEW IDEAS?

In a nutshell, it's *provocation*. Here's why.

Please imagine for a moment that the surface of our brains is a little like a landscape or, more specifically, a mountain.

When information comes into our brains through our five senses – i.e. sight, sound, smell, taste and touch – what happens is very similar to a raincloud hovering over that mountain, releasing drops of rain.

New drops of information, like rainfall, will naturally follow the path of least resistance. And here lies the problem.

The more we think in a particular way, the more likely we are to think that way in the future, because new information will simply flow down the same old neural pathways which have grown deeper and wider with use.

'And your point is?' you may well ask. My point is that, like it or not, human beings are essentially creatures of habit. Over 80 per cent of what we do today is almost identical to what we did yesterday (and will go on to do tomorrow), from the way we brush our teeth, to the journey we take to work. To be honest, we couldn't function in our day-to-day lives if this wasn't the case, because we'd be too busy trying to re-invent the wheel.

If we want to think creatively, however, habitual thinking is incredibly unhelpful. Creativity is all about creating fresh patterns, not repeating familiar ones. Or as Edward de Bono describes it…

'The brain is a superb pattern-making and pattern-using system, which is why it is so *bad* at creativity… We have the ability to think in new patterns, but our minds are optimized to think with existing patterns.'

And that's why we need *provocation* to jolt the system. Provocation can help our minds to escape old patterns of thinking and behaviour, by re-directing the rivers of thought, or as the innovation company What-if put it, to 'River Jump'!

## 7  BUT IN REALITY, ISN'T BUSINESS CREATIVITY JUST ABOUT MARKETING AND NEW PRODUCT DEVELOPMENT?

Not any more.

These days, virtually all parts of all businesses can benefit from a healthy dose of **Cunningly Clever Creativity**:

➜ Senior managers can use it to help them envision their strategic goals.

→ Middle managers can use it to solve operational problems 'laterally'.

→ Junior managers can use it to find new ways for engaging their teams.

So it really doesn't matter that much if you work in Finance or IT, HR or Customer Services. If you want to improve what you do – whether it's systems and structures, or processes and procedures – the chances are you'll need some fresh ideas to help you do it.

Oh, by the way, if by chance you happen to think that creative thinking is only applicable to certain 'types' of businesses, please think again.

Over the years as a Creative Change Agent I have had the good fortune to work with all types of organisations, from banks to airlines and mobile phone companies to TV companies. Some have been very large, some very small. Some private sector, some public sector. Along the way I've even ended up working with rocket scientists, nuclear physicists, mining engineers, heads of oncology departments and, yes, even chartered accountants. The reason I am sharing this with you is simple. What I've found is that there is barely a business on this planet that doesn't need to innovate, and to keep innovating, if it wants to survive and thrive in a rapidly changing world. And that is why **Cunningly Clever Creativity** has never been more important.

Phew! That wasn't too painful was it?

Now we've got that out of the way, let's focus on the more practical bit.

Before we do, however, two more points.

Firstly, nobody has a monopoly on good ideas. That's right – *nobody*. Anyone can come up with them, at any time, and the good news is that you don't have to be amazingly creative to do so, and you often don't have to be an expert either. Far from it.

According to Dr Harry Alder in his book *Train Your Brain*, and Professor John Adair in his book *The Art of Creative Thinking*, '46 out of 58 of the major twentieth-century inventions were invented by people in the *wrong* business.' This extensive list includes the Gillette throwaway razor (which was invented by a cork salesman), FedEx (which was started by a combat fighter who had fought in Vietnam), and Dunlop tyres (which was invented by a vet from Belfast), and so it goes on… the automated telephone exchange (undertaker), Biro (bank clerk), and the photocopier (lawyer). Even a journalist invented the parking meter but, then again, they would, wouldn't they.

Secondly, I think it was Charles Handy – the famous management guru – who once said, 'Remember the stories, forget the examples.' The same applies here.

Please don't get hung up on the petty details of 'But I've never heard of this business before' or 'But what on earth has this UK business got to do with my business in the USA, Australia, Germany, Japan, China, or India?' Or perhaps the worst of all, 'But that company's gone bust, hasn't it? Ha, so much for their **Cunningly Clever Creativity**!'

The **Cunningly Clever Creativity** examples in this book are simply intended to inspire you so you can have more **Genius Moments** in your professional life.

Like a ladder, use them to help you climb up to new levels of success within your own business, and then get rid of the ladder…

# HOW TO GET THE MOST OUT OF THE REST OF THIS BOOK

**'In order to attain the impossible, one must attempt the absurd.'**

Cervantes

n a moment you'll be introduced to 26 different idea-generation tools for helping you to boost your business success.

How you choose to read the section is, of course, entirely up to you.

Here are a few suggestions:

→ You may prefer to focus on only 'one' specific tool at a time, using it to stimulate fresh ideas instantly.

→ You may prefer to thumb through the pages, and then pick a letter or theme which particularly intrigues or inspires you.

→ You may prefer to dip in and out (as you would with any reference book), depending on your mood, your need and the time you have available. For example, maybe the next time you've got a corporate brainstorm coming up, and you'd love a few handy tips on how to get your group thinking above and beyond the usual tired old solutions.

→ You may prefer to be brave and read the whole thing in one go (bet you can't!). If you do, however, please bear in mind that there's a lot of **Cunningly Clever Creativity** information crammed into these pages, so please be prepared for your head feeling totally overwhelmed by the end of it.

→ You may even prefer to use it as nothing more than a coffee mat, or a prop for keeping the door open so you can get a nice through-draught.

That's cunningly creative.

Like any toolbox, the tools inside it are simply a means to an end, not an end in themselves. It's what you *do* with them that matters – so always keep a pen and paper or laptop nearby, for jotting down whatever ideas spring to mind as a result of using them, from the beautiful to the bonkers, and the brilliant to the bizarre...

However, if you genuinely want to make sure that these **Genius Tools** benefit your work and your business as much as possible, I strongly recommend you follow these **5 Golden Guidelines**.

# THE 5 GOLDEN GUIDELINES FOR USING CUNNINGLY CLEVER CREATIVITY TO GENERATE IDEAS

## 1 BE SPECIFIC

Before you invest precious time and energy generating new ideas, you need to be crystal clear – or at least a lot clearer than mud – about precisely what it is you're hoping **Cunningly Clever Creativity** can help you to achieve. For example, 'My goal (or our goal) is to…'

→ 'Double sales in 12 months'

→ 'Cut costs by 30 per cent (in a way that cuts fat, not muscle)'

→ 'Come up with a new brand name for this product'

→ 'Motivate and engage my team more effectively'

→ 'Re-design this process/system so it becomes twice as efficient'

→ 'Create and formulate a new strategic plan for the business'.

To be honest, it doesn't really matter what you decide to go with, as long as it matters to *you*. All we're saying here is that it's rather like putting a postal address on the front of an envelope. The more specific you can be about where you're heading the better, and the more likely you are to get there.

## 2 KEEP SEPARATE

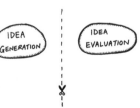

Always remember to keep *idea generation* separate from *idea evaluation*.

Why? Because trying to do both at the same time simply won't work.

Idea generation is all about 'divergent thinking' (thinking outwards to explore what could be), whereas idea evaluation is all about 'convergent thinking' (thinking inwards to scrutinise what is).

The tools you'll discover in the next section are all about idea generation (*not* idea evaluation) so, in this respect, anything goes, and the more the merrier. No idea is too weird or wacky, so make sure you write them all down as they emerge.

---

**'Step one is to create, step two is to edit. The problem is people try to do both at once, and the brain can't cope... Shall I write hobgoblin? No. Demon? No. Both? Neither? You've got to work backwards from where you need to be.'**

Quincy Jones (Legendary music producer)

---

## 3  NO BUTS

Linked to the last point, it's vital at this stage that you suspend all *buts*. This is because the word 'but' is not only an idea evaluation word, *but* it also happens to be the No. 1 idea killer:

→ 'But it won't work'

→ 'But it's been done before'

→ 'But that's stupid'

→ 'But it'll cause offence'

→ 'But it'll cost too much'

→ 'But it'll take too long'

→ 'But I'll look a fool if I suggest it'.

The following section of the book is not about coming up with perfectly polished ideas, or finished ideas, it's about coming up with 'beginning ideas'.

The improvement of them, and refinement of them, will happen at a later stage in the process. That means you will get a chance to say 'but' later. In fact, it's very important that you do. But not just yet…

## 4 CRAZY'S GOOD

Often, hidden within a crazy idea, there is a useful principle which can provide us with the solution we are looking for. For example, many years ago Edward de Bono was asked by the police to help reduce crime levels in the UK.

Someone in the session came up with the idea, 'What if policemen had six eyes?' How ludicrous. Policemen will never have six eyes. However, what about the idea within the idea? What if policemen could have more eyes? What if policemen could have eyes on the street even when they're back at the station? What if they could look through other people's eyes? And this way of thinking allegedly led to Citizen's Watch, which later become Neighbourhood Watch.

Once again, if we evaluate too prematurely, we can end up overlooking the diamond in the rough…

# 5 KEEP MOVING

Similarly, you might find yourself coming up with an idea that's so crazy you can't even find the useful principle within it, and so you're sorely tempted to throw it in the bin straight away.

If this happens, however, please don't give up. 'Roll with it', as rock stars often say. For example, I recently facilitated a workshop for a company to help them run more effective meetings. In the middle of it someone came up with the crazy idea of, 'How about we get our mums to do it?'

As you might expect, to begin with there was a little laugh, but often wherever there's a laugh there's a good idea.

All too easily this idea could have been stopped dead in its tracks. But by keeping the process moving, this idea led to the idea of 'Mum's the word', which led to the idea of perhaps offering more 'confidential' meetings where people felt safe enough to say what was really on their mind, rather than simply communicating at a very superficial level.

So, if possible, let ideas *bounce*. For example, on the face of it, growing a catering business might have nothing to do with the movie star John Wayne. But 'John Wayne' might encourage you to think of cowboys, and cowboys might encourage you to think of 'branding' and, before you know it, you're deciding to re-design your whole branding strategy. Or maybe you'll find your thoughts 'bounce' from cowboys to Texas, and Texas to oil, and then motor oil to olive oil, and... well, let's move on to those terribly helpful idea-generation tools.

# THE CUNNINGLY CLEVER CREATIVITY TOOLKIT

'To the man who only has a hammer in his toolkit, every problem looks like a nail.'

Abraham Maslow (Genius psychologist)

# ANALOGY

If you are looking for a new idea to help you improve your business's products, services or performance, you might want to use the **analogy** technique. Simply take your mind on a journey to a parallel world – like Ancient Rome or the Starship *Enterprise* – and apply back fresh insights to your unique situation.

For example, 'nature' has often been used to help people solve problems creatively. That is why we have the London Underground (inspired by the shipworm), angle-poised lamps (inspired by the movements of the human arm), and the ring-pull on a Coke can (inspired by peeling a banana). So next time you are snacking your lunch in the park, keep an open mind. If skimming stones on a lake could give rise to the dambusters, and sticky burrs to Velcro, then perhaps the answer you are looking for is much closer than you think…

ANALOGY DOODLE...

BRUNEL'S SUSPENSION BRIDGE

SYDNEY OPERA HOUSE

CATS' EYES

## CUNNINGLY CLEVER CREATIVITY NUGGET

**S**everal years ago I met an entrepreneur called Rachel Lowe. She explained that for many years she'd been a taxi driver struggling to make ends meet, and then one day it suddenly struck her that driving people around all over the place was rather like 'a board game'. Now some people might have made this **analogy** and then left it at that. Rachel, however, decided to take it one step further. She created a board game about taxi drivers driving people all around well-known cities to visit major tourist attractions, calling the games 'Destination Dublin', 'Destination London', and so on. Her 'Destination' games became highly successful – even outselling Monopoly in many stores – and at its peak her business, RTL Games, was turning over millions each year.

## TURNING THEORY INTO PRACTICE

**1** Think of a current business issue you face. If you were to compare it with something else, what might that something else be? Is it like fighting a battle, wrestling with alligators, or possibly even playing football for a team that's 3:0 down? Whatever your answer, have a go at using your metaphor to spark new ideas and solutions. Perhaps ask yourself what others might do if they were standing in your shoes, such as Napoleon, Crocodile Dundee or David Beckham…

**2** Pick up a dictionary and choose a word at random. It doesn't really matter which word, as long as it's a noun. So go for something like a 'sword', a 'horse' or a 'pyramid'. Now imagine that this word contains the answer you are looking for – the key to you achieving greater business success. What can it teach you? For example, maybe it's encouraging you to wonder,

'What if my business objectives could be made as sharp as a sword?' or 'What if, like the horse-whisperer, I could learn to trust my intuition and become a more effective leader?'

**❸** Use any device you like for creating unusal and unexpected **analogies**. For example, spin a globe, and pick a country, such as Brazil. Then wonder what might happen if you could make your business as popular and exciting with your customers as a Rio carnival. Or use what the company Synectics calls a 'career excursion'. Reflect on how your business challenge might be overcome by a firefighter, a chef, a spy or a ballet dancer. If you were a gardener, for example, what seeds would need to be planted to help grow your business, and what weeds would need to be pulled up?

---

## THINKSPIRATION
## 'You can find inspiration in everything and, if you can't, look again.'
Paul Smith (Designer)

---

# BISOCIATION

This creative thinking technique is all about combining 'two or more' different elements to create something new.

Take Gillette, for example. What happened when they combined two single razors? They created the double-razor. What happened when they added one more? The triple razor. What happened when they added aloe vera, safety strips and batteries? Innovation after innovation after innovation.

So, if you are on the quest for new business ideas, why not ask yourself, 'What might happen if we mix this with that?' such as connecting your marketing strategy with 'red roses' or even a 'fire extinguisher'. Yes, it might sound crazy at first, but the end results could be extremely fruitful. After all, Saga Holidays came about from mixing *travel + the older generation*; skateboards from *wheels + wood*; and Facebook from *connectivity + the internet*... Or what about Kinder Surprise Eggs, which combined 'chocolate' with 'toys', and 'eating' and 'playing', and went on to become one of the best-selling sweets of all time...

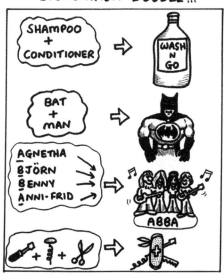

BISOCIATION DOODLE...

SHAMPOO + CONDITIONER ⇨ WASH N GO

BAT + MAN ⇨

AGNETHA
BJÖRN
BENNY
ANNI-FRID ⇨ ABBA

⤬ + ⬡ + ✂ ⇨

## CUNNINGLY CLEVER CREATIVITY NUGGET

**A**lthough we might take printed books for granted these days, hundreds of years ago there weren't many books around for people to read because reproduction was usually done by hand (and often by monks). Then in 1440 a man called Johannes Gutenberg used some **Cunningly Clever Creativity** to **bisociate**. He wondered what might happen if he combined certain mechanical features of a wine-press with certain mechanical features of a coin-press. As a result, he invented 'movable type', and not only spawned a whole new printing industry, but also helped to radically transform the world we live in.

## TURNING THEORY INTO PRACTICE

❶ Ask yourself what might happen if you could combine any of these elements into your business to help create something new:

➔ **Dinosaur** (Think of the merchandise success Spielberg enjoyed as a result of combining dinosaurs with the film industry in the movie *Jurassic Park*.)

➔ **Bubbles** (Think of the success Jacob Schweppe enjoyed in 1741 when he came up with the idea of deliberately carbonating water, giving rise to the fizzy drinks industry.)

➔ **Newspapers** (Think of the success of *The Week* magazine, which scans newspaper articles all around the world each week to combine the most interesting or useful bits, and give readers 'all you need to know about everything that matters'.)

❷ Take a look at your business as a whole, and then ask yourself what might happen if you were able to combine different parts of it – different functions, different people, different tasks. For example, closer integration between different departments can often help to boost productivity in a business by diminishing the disadvantages of a 'silo mentality'.

❸ Open your mind to numerous forms of **bisociation** (like a smartphone) and then ask yourself what you could potentially learn from them. Take, for example, an aircraft carrier (= a ship + aircrafts). These ships enable fighter jets to be taken all over the world... What if you could take what you do all over the world, even to places you have not considered yet? What if you could 'land' new business opportunities just as quickly or effectively? What if you could combine specific qualities of a ship (such as a propeller) or an aircraft (such as radar) to your business to help you reach your aspirations?

**B**

---

## THINKSPIRATION
## 'The human brain is a giant association machine.'
Tony Buzan

---

# Clever copycat

**B**izarrely enough, one of the best ways for coming up with innovative business ideas is *not* to come up with innovative business ideas! Simply borrow other people's, making sure you give them your own original twist (to avoid complex legal issues).

Starbucks, for example, did not invent the coffee shop. They simply borrowed the Milan espresso bar concept, and gave it a modern American touch. Similarly, when Simon Woodroffe created YO! Sushi, he applied the conveyor-belt restaurant idea from Japan to a new context – the UK.

So, before you waste time and resources trying to re-invent the wheel, how about 'modelling' the success of others. Boyzone did with Take That; Oasis did with the Beatles; John Madjeski – the founder of *Auto Trader* – allegedly did after noticing an American car magazine which used 'crude photography', and ended up selling his business for £260 million…

CLEVER COPYCAT DOODLE…

## CUNNINGLY CLEVER CREATIVITY NUGGET

In the late 1800s a Scotsman called Thomas Blake Glover (who later became known as 'The Scottish Samurai') introduced a range of innovative Western industrial ideas to Japan, ranging from the locomotive to the mechanical coal mine. These were not his inventions or his ideas. He simply 'borrowed' these concepts and, as a result, ended up having a hugely influential role in the development of the modern Japanese economy. Companies like the Kirin Brewery Company and the Mitsubishi Corporation, for example, originated from Glover's gift for being a **clever copycat** ...

## TURNING THEORY INTO PRACTICE

❶ Take a moment to think about two or three businesses that have become immensely successful (regardless of whether or not they are similar to your own). What could you potentially learn from them, or 'borrow' from them, and then apply back to your own unique situation? For example, what if you could 'model' elements of Coca-Cola's amazing distribution network? Or 'model' Apple's eye for innovative design?

❷ How about investing a little more time online researching what other businesses like yours are up to around the world? As the Thomas Blake Glover example shows, if something works well in one country, it could (with a little tweaking here and there) work in another.

❸ What if you stopped thinking of **clever copycat** as pinching someone else's idea, and started seeing it as being inspired by someone else's idea? After all, the film *Apocalypse Now* might never have happened if it hadn't been 'inspired' by Joseph Conrad's novel *Heart of Darkness*; Italian spaghetti might never have happened if it hadn't been 'inspired' by the noodles Marco Polo came across on his travels to China; and John Bird's magazine *The Big Issue* (which helps the homeless in the UK) might never have happened if he and his business partner hadn't been 'inspired' by the magazine *Street News* which they spotted by accident on a trip to New York…

---

## THINKSPIRATION
### 'All the songs have already been written. All you can do is re-write them.'
Noel Gallagher

---

# DELETE

Time and time again, people in business focus on what they need to do, rather than on what they need to *stop* doing. This is why the **delete** creative thinking technique can be so powerful.

Many business breakthroughs have come about by individuals asking provocative questions like, 'What if we simplify this?' or 'What if we eliminate this altogether?'

For example, back in 1958, Jack Kilby of Texas Instruments wondered why the electrical circuit he was working on needed over 30 different component parts. 'What if it only had one?' he asked himself, and went on to invent the silicon chip! Likewise, back in 1979, Sony Chairman Akio Morita saw the potential of a tape recorder which did 'not' record, and successfully went on to launch the Walkman. Yup. Sometimes less is more. That is why First Direct **deleted** high street banks, and Dyson **deleted** 'the bag'…

DELETE DOODLE …

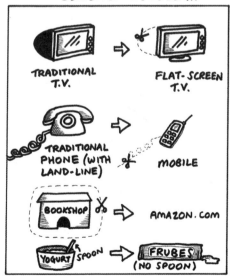

**H**istorically, the only way of preserving fruit juice was with alcohol. Then, in 1867, along came a Scottish shipbuilder called Lauchlan Rose who used the **delete** creative thinking tool to ask the question, 'What if we could do the same thing without alcohol?' In the process, he came up an alternative method for preserving fruit juice, and his famous Rose's Lime Juice became the 'world's first concentrated fruit drink'.

## TURNING THEORY INTO PRACTICE

**❶** Imagine what might happen if you **deleted** a certain aspect of your business – maybe a feature of your product, a service you provide, or perhaps even a particular time-wasting activity like pointless meetings. But please don't just pick the obvious things. Look at everything you do and then wonder, 'Is this strictly necessary?' Not long ago, for example, the pop star Mick Hucknall asked himself, 'Do I really need a record company?' and after concluding he probably didn't, he then went on to set up his own label for releasing new Simply Red material, so he could keep the lion's share of the profits.

**❷** Please take a moment to dwell on the word **delete**. What images spring to mind? Erasers rubbing out pencil drawings? Editors throwing away the waffle? Hairdressers trimming hair? As you do so, learn to see in what ways leaving things out, or cutting things back, could have far more of a positive influence on your business than a negative one. Look at how successful McDonald's became, for example, from being a restaurant 'without' any washing-up to do. Or look at how B&Q prospered from the D.I.Y. concept, enabling homeowners to do repairs 'without' the help of professional builders or carpenters. Or look at companies that have thrived on 'just-in-time' delivery, which **deletes** the need for large warehouses to store items for long periods of time.

❸ Look at what your competitors do, and then consider what might happen if you could achieve the same (or maybe better) results *without* doing it. When Google started out, for example, they didn't spend a fortune on advertising and marketing like many others… they **deleted** this approach, and focused on word-of-mouth instead, and they are now the fourth biggest company in the USA.

## THINKSPIRATION
### 'Put all your eggs in one basket, and then watch the basket.'
Andrew Carnegie (the American billionaire industrialist who used to be involved in a variety of businesses, before **deleting** the bulk of his options to focus on just one)

# ENLARGE

Sometimes, if you are stuck for solutions in business, you might find it helpful to think big. REALLY BIG.

By magnifying your ideas, and asking questions like, 'What if we could stretch or expand this?' or 'What would we do if we were the largest company in the world?', suddenly you can pole-vault your mind to a new level of possibilities.

After all, **enlargement** is why we now have everything from toy shops like Toys R Us, to products like wide-screen TVs, and services like stretched limos for hire. It is also why Mark Bolan came up with the name T-Rex, because – like the dinosaur – he wanted to become the 'biggest thing on the planet'.

When using this technique, however, please take care. The *Titanic* was an **enlarged** ship, and Live Aid was an **enlarged** pop concert: same thinking, big difference.

## ENLARGE DOODLE...

## CUNNINGLY CLEVER CREATIVITY NUGGET

In many ways it could be argued that one can of sweetcorn tastes much like another. Possibly the most famous brand of all, however, Green Giant, was the brainchild of advertising legend Leo Burnett who came up with this gigantic green character to help differentiate the product back in 1928. Inspired by the name of an unusually large pea called the 'Green Giant', Burnett converted this into the famous 'Ho, ho, ho' Jolly Green Giant who appeared as a 'smiling green-skinned giant wearing a tunic, wreath and boots made of leaves'. Burnett firmly believed that 'share of market' could only be built on 'share of mind': by using **enlarged** thinking he was able to create an instantly recognisable and memorable harvest-god image which could be 'engraved on the consciousness' of consumers...

# E

## TURNING THEORY INTO PRACTICE

**❶** Take a moment to consider what might happen if you could suddenly wave a magic wand like Merlin and **enlarge** either a part of, or all of, your business. What if you could suddenly make it 10 times bigger, or 100 times bigger, or even 1,000 times bigger? What difference might such a shift in scale potentially have on your profile, or the impact you have on your clients or customers?

**❷** Make a long list of all the benefits you associate with size. For example, being tall can be a huge advantage when playing basketball. Alternatively, wearing a massive Mexican hat can provide extra shade in the midday sun. Then ask yourself in what ways your business could potentially prosper if you were able to expand it or stretch it in a similar way? Could it help you to 'reach' more customers? Could it help you to 'protect' your business from a variety of harmful 'financial' rays?

**③** What if you could challenge some of your self-limiting beliefs and stop thinking small? Like the famous story *The Frog in the Well*, ask yourself what might happen if you could start climbing out of the well your business is currently in, and start exploring the wider world out there, with all its exciting possibilities and opportunities…

---

## THINKSPIRATION
### 'I like thinking big. If you're going to be thinking anything, you might as well think big.'
Donald Trump

---

# FUTURE THINKING

One of the five main uses of business creativity – according to lateral thinking guru Edward de Bono – is **future thinking**. In other words, 'seeing' where we want to get to, long before we get there.

Some managers achieve this by literally drawing their desired outcome. Others prefer to imagine they are being interviewed by a journalist in three years' time, who remarks, 'Wow, what a success story! How on earth did you do it?'

The key point to remember here is that envisioning is *not* the same as daydreaming. Daydreaming involves 'escaping reality', whereas envisioning involves 'transforming' it. That is why it is no coincidence that many of the world's leading companies also have the most compelling visions, such as Apple's 'Making computers fun'. It is also why Peter Drucker once said, 'The best way to predict the future, is to create it'…

## FUTURE THINKING DOODLE...

## CUNNINGLY CLEVER CREATIVITY NUGGET

There is a famous story Antony Robbins tells of a man being shown around a newly opened Disney theme park by Roy Disney (shortly after Walt Disney had died). 'What a shame your father isn't here to see it,' says the man. 'On the contrary,' replies Walt Disney's son, 'it's because he saw it that it's here today'...

## TURNING THEORY INTO PRACTICE

**❶** If you were to picture the future of your business in 2 or 5 or 10 years' time, what would you want that picture to look like? What successes would you ultimately want to have achieved? What images spring to mind? Please don't worry too much about getting carried away because, in this context, getting carried away is OK. A vision is meant to be ambitious and exciting, and bold and bright, so that, like the stars, we can use it to help us navigate our course. So, for example, although Microsoft's vision of 'a personal computer in every home' may never become complete reality, Microsoft has definitely taken huge strides to shift the world in this direction.

**❷** You may want to take the process one stage further and actually draw your vision on a large piece of paper. If you do, however, please don't get hung up on your artistic ability – it is really not important. To borrow a slightly cheesy phrase, 'It's the think, not the ink' that matters. So doodle away to your heart's content. Time and again in business, as in other walks of life, 'seeing is achieving'. So, as Steven Covey puts it, 'Always begin with the end in mind'.

③ Alternatively, how about taking Walt Disney's advice of 'If you can dream it, you can do it' literally and actually close your eyes for a power nap? (Obviously not while you're driving!) As you mentally visualise, perhaps reflect on the following questions: What would you most want to *see* happening in your business? What would you most want to *hear* being said? Then, if possible, make your experience even more sensory-specific by asking yourself how this type of success might also *feel*, *smell* or *taste*. Use your dream like a magnet, to draw you closer towards it…

## THINKSPIRATION
### 'Capital isn't scarce. Vision is.'
Sam Walton (founder of Walmart)

# GOAT

If something really annoys you, or 'gets your goat', don't despair. Why? Because from a business point of view, you might have inadvertantly struck gold.

Many successful businesses and inventions began because people got really fed up by someone or something. Avis, for example, started after William Avis got increasingly irritated that he was unable to rent a car whenever he stepped off a plane, and he was always a long taxi-ride away from where he needed to get to. Similarly, Frank McNamara set up Diner Club (the world's first credit card) after the immense embarrassment he felt when he got up to pay for his meal in an expensive New York restaurant and suddenly realised he'd left his wallet behind and he had no cash on him.

So, why not take the design consultancy Ideo's advice and keep a 'bug list' of all the things that wind you up or get you down? The theory is that if it bugs *you*, it'll probably bug others too and, if you can help to fix their problem, they'll often be only too happy to pay you for it. This is why many self-help gurus like to tell us that an 'irritation is information'. And as words of wisdom go, how irritating is that?

GOAT DOODLE...

I HATE IT WHEN...

MY COAT GETS SMELLY IN THE RAIN! SNIFF

CHARLES MACINTOSH

THE MACINTOSH (1823)

DUST MAKES ME SNEEZE!

JAMES SPANGLER

THE HOOVER (1908)

## CUNNINGLY CLEVER CREATIVITY NUGGET

In 1843 an insurance broker missed out on a highly lucrative deal because his pen failed to work properly. By the time he returned with a pen that did work, it was too late. Someone had pipped him to the post, and encouraged the client to sign their contract instead. In true **goat** style, the broker was furious. So furious, in fact, that he started to take a closer look at the design of the failing pen, and decided he could do better. As a result, Lewis Edison Waterman left the insurance business, and Waterman pens soon became famous all around the world...

# TURNING THEORY INTO PRACTICE

❶ In a business context, what are you particularly angry about? What isn't right? What gets under your skin? What secretly drives you mad?

→ Have you had enough of being sent endless, pointless e-mails?

→ Is there a lack of joined-up thinking?

→ Are your processes and systems worryingly out of date?

Often, clearly identifying what 'bugs' you, others in your company, or especially your customers, can be a useful first step on the road to discovering innovative solutions.

❷ Time and again, anger is perceived in a negative way. Anger, however, can also be an amazingly positive force, too: a force for good, a force for change, and a force for bouncing back from setbacks. It is important to acknowledge that anger is a natural emotion (like sadness, happiness and fear) and remember that anger itself never hurt anybody. It's what we do with our anger that counts. So, why not use your 'anger' as fuel, to help you get from where your business is, to where you want your business to be?

❸ What if you could draw inspiration from other people in business who have used their anger to go on to achieve great things? Take Conrad Nicholson Hilton, for example, who back in 1919 was so annoyed that the bank he wanted to buy had been pushed beyond his price range, that he promptly went off to spend a night in a hotel, and ended up buying the hotel instead…

---

## THINKSPIRATION
### 'Innovation comes from angry and driven people.'
Tom Peters

---

# Halo

The 'halo' creative thinking technique is all about generating ideas for *good* business. It's as if you're standing in the shoes of (or perhaps even sandles of) a spiritual guru, and asking the question, 'How can we be more kind, caring, or giving, in a ruthlessly commercial world?'

Take Anita Roddick, for example, whose ethical approach to fairly traded cosmetics and persistent avoidance of tests on animals, ended up with her Body Shop empire branching out into over 50 countries, and eventually being sold for £650 million! Or the TV chef Jamie Oliver, whose profitable Fifteen restaurant concept gives disadvantaged youths the chance to release their potential by training to become masters of 'Pukka' cuisine.

**Halo**, however, is a versatile tool, and is not the exclusive property of social entrepreneurs.

Large organisations, for example, might want to use it to help them maximise the win–win benefits of corporate social responsibility. Similarly, the modern manager might want to use it to foster a happier working environment, based on the view that happier people tend to work more productively than those who are deeply miserable (as Quaker families like Cadbury and Rowntree realised long ago).

So why not use **halo** to help you open your mind up to 'the power of nice'? Let's face it, in business as in life, often the best way to help ourselves is to help others, too…

# HALO DOODLE...

| | | |
|---|---|---|
| CAR | ⇨ | **"A CAR FOR EVERYONE."** (FORD MOTOR Co.) 1906 |
| PHONE | ⇨ | **"IT'S GOOD TO TALK."** (B.T. ADVERTISING CAMPAIGN 1994) |
| COFFEE | ⇨ | **"FAIRTRADE COFFEE"** (MAX HAVELAAR) NETHERLANDS: 1988 |

## CUNNINGLY CLEVER CREATIVITY NUGGET

In July 2007 the pop star Prince decided to 'give' his new album away for free in *The Mail on Sunday*, as part of a newspaper special offer (much to the anger and irritation of the music industry). Whatever his motives might have been, one thing is for sure. As a result of his **halo** thinking, his album – which cynics say might not have sold too well anyway, or made much money because of modern piracy issues – suddenly became international news. All over the world his act of creative rebellion captured the headlines and drew huge attention to his upcoming tour. Largely on the back of this publicity he ended up selling out at the O2 stadium in London for 22 nights running!

# TURNING THEORY INTO PRACTICE

**❶** Marketeers have known for many years about the advantages of giving away freebies: free magazines, free holidays, free gym membership. Of course, this does not mean that they are being charitable or altruistic. It simply means that they recognise it makes good business sense to raise awareness of what's on sale, and also to trade on the 'principle of reciprocity' (i.e. you scratch my back and I'll scratch yours). So, with this in mind, how about using **halo** to ask yourself the question, 'What could I potentially give away to help attract new business?'

**❷** Regardless of whether you're self-employed or work for a large corporation, the chances are that your ability to 'network' is an amazingly important skill. **Halo** helps to remind us that the best networkers in life are not those who thrust their business card into someone's hand at a wedding with an expectant look on their face. Truly successful networkers are 'givers' rather than 'takers': people who realise that networking is about the giving, sharing and gathering of information, for mutual advantage. So maybe consider, 'Who could I potentially introduce to this person to help them in *their* business?' or 'Who do I know who could add value to what *they* do?' (And ultimately do this without expecting anything in return.)

**❸** What if you began to adopt an 'abundancy mindset', and started to perceive the world and universe around you as an infinite source of wealth? Admittedly this might sound a little on the tree-hugging hippy side (and what's wrong with that?), but it can also help to make 'giving' thoughts a great deal easier in a commercial context…

# THINKSPIRATION
## 'What helps people, helps business.'
Leo Burnett

# INDIANA JONES

The **Indiana Jones** technique invites us to look at business through the eyes of a child. This isn't to say it wants us to be childish. On the contrary. All it wants us to be is 'childlike', because often it's the 'big kids' of the commercial world – like Sir Richard Branson and Steve Jobs – who generate the most innovative ideas.

One way of using this technique is to reflect on happy experiences from our own childhood. This, for example, is precisely what the film producer George Lucas did when he modelled **Indiana Jones** on the cliffhanger adventure stories he had grown up with as a boy (Indiana, by the way, was named after his pet dog).

A second way is to think of children as 'wise sages' who can teach us all we need to know (if we'd only listen to them!). When a man called Edward Land, for example, took a photograph of his daughter back in 1943 and she impatiently asked, 'Why can't I see it now?', Land started to ask himself the same question, and promptly went on to invent the Polaroid camera.

A third way, is to imagine anything and everything we might associate with 'child's play' – from toy trains to marble runs, and Harry Potter to Peter Pan – because when it comes to solving problems and doing things differently, this can often provide us with a never-ending source of creative inspiration…

**INDIANA JONES DOODLE…**

STOP KIDDING AROUND!

DOMINOES ⇨ BRAILLE

SPINNING TOP ⇨ GUGGENHEIM MUSEUM, N.Y.

TUBE ⇨ STETHOSCOPE (RENÉ LAËNNEC: 1816)

**A**s we all know, children have a tremendous gift for asking challenging questions (usually beginning with the word 'why'). Back in 1971, however, Roger Hargreaves's 7-year-old son Adam was to ask him a question that would not only change his life, but also turn him into a multi-millionaire. The question was 'What does a tickle look like?' and, as Hargreaves began to draw a funny round orange figure with ludicrously long arms and a blue hat, he set in motion what is now known as the *Mr Men* series, selling 100 million books worldwide.

# TURNING THEORY INTO PRACTICE

**❶** If you could take a step back from your current business activities, and view what's going on from a child's perspective, what would you notice? Would it all make sense or would it seem unnecessarily complicated? Would you find it boring or cool? Better still – as a management consultant from Kids Plc – what might you advise to help them sort this business out?

**❷** For what it's worth, I believe that *creativity = permission*. That's why it's no coincidence that the leading innovative companies on the planet – such as Apple, Google and 3M – also happen to have the highest levels of 'permission': the permission to think new thoughts, the permission to challenge the status quo, and the permission to make 'excusable' mistakes from time to time. These are companies that are fully aware that creativity can easily get killed by too many rules and regulations, and too much structure and hierarchy. In a word, too much 'parent'. So, with this in mind, you might want to reflect on your own organisational culture, and ask yourself to what extent innovative thinking and behaviour are encouraged or discouraged. Put simply, are your people given enough trust?

At the UK smoothie company Innocent a permissive approach is taken to the extreme. Their whole culture revolves around the **Indiana Jones** technique, from the witty wording on their bottles to the fact that their offices have artificial grass instead of carpets, and the pictures on the walls of the management team are not of them as serious adults but as they were when they were kids.

❸ Sir Richard Branson has always lived by the principle of 'Make Work Fun'. How much more productive or profitable might your business be if you could do the same?

---

## THINKSPIRATION
### 'The greatest thing in life is to keep your mind young.'
Henry Ford

---

# JUMBLE-IT-UP

The **jumble-it-up** creative thinking technique works rather like a poker player shuffling a deck of cards. Put simply, it's a rearranging tool that encourages us to ask the question, 'What if we put the same parts in a different order?'

Look at the world of games, for example, and you'll find that many products, from Lego to Meccano and even the Rubik's cube, involve **jumble-it-up** in some shape or form. (In fact, it is said that there are actually 915 million different ways it's possible to combine just 6 pieces of Lego!) Or what about the protection business where this technique has been used to create all kinds of inventions, from the 'Enigma Machine' for protecting secrets, to 'combination locks' for protecting possessions. Having said this, however, please don't assume that the **jumble-it-up** technique always has to be product-related.

In an organisational context, for example, it could be used to **jumble up** hierarchy, so a CEO periodically goes 'back to the shop floor' to find out what's really going on in the business. Alternatively, it could be used to **jumble up** time, so what normally goes at the end of a sequence goes at the beginning (or vice versa). This is evidently how the insurance company Prudential came up with the idea of paying out life insurance before people died, in what became known as 'living needs benefits'.

So, next time you feel stuck in a rut, why not see your situation like a kaleidoscope, and give it a shake to create a whole new pattern?

## JUMBLE-IT-UP DOODLE...

## CUNNINGLY CLEVER CREATIVITY NUGGET

**B**ack in the 1950s, during the filming of a black and white TV series called *The Adventures of Robin Hood*, the production team was faced with the challenge of building lots of different sets for different scenes: a castle one minute, a church the next, and perhaps an inn from time to time, too. What made it worse was that they also had to do this very quickly (with a new half-hour episode being filmed every four to five days) and on a limited budget! Luckily their art director Peter Proud used a little **Cunningly Clever Creativity** to come up with a solution. It suddenly dawned on him that, if they put the props on wheels, the same parts could be **jumbled up** to create all kinds of new and interesting scenes, both quickly and cost-effectively, and, as a result, they went on to make 143 highly profitable episodes...

# TURNING THEORY INTO PRACTICE

**❶** Give yourself a moment to list as many different 'sequences' as you can in your business, or at least the part of your business most relevant to you. For example, one sequence might be a *chain* like a chain of command or a supply chain; another might be a *schedule* such as '11.15am is the time we normally do X', or 'Tuesday is the day we normally do Y'. Once you've done that, work through your list, and then, one by one, ask yourself what might happen if you whirled it around. For example, suppose you could help your team have their 'Thank God it's Friday' feeling on a Monday? Or suppose you could improve your time management by making the bulk of your daily phone calls in one chunk, rather than randomly spread throughout the day?

**❷** Like a maestro who uses a finite number of black and white notes on a piano to create an infinite variety of tunes, what if you could **jumble up** the different parts of your business to play new chords? For example, many of the world's most innovative organisations like Google actively encourage different departments and individuals of varying levels of seniority to mix with one another at mealtimes, which can help to avoid silo thinking by boosting the cross-fertilisation of ideas.

**❸** How about writing down separate parts of a business process on separate strips of paper, and then seeing what happens when you switch them all around? Yes, the end result might be gobbledegook, but this is also how David Bowie used to write his lyrics, and it certainly did him no harm...

---

# THINKSPIRATION
## 'There are only 3 colors, 10 digits, and 7 notes; it's what we do with them that's important.'
Jim Rohn

---

# Kiss

The **K.I.S.S**. technique stands for 'Keep it *so* simple', with the emphasis on *so*. Why? Because, as we all know, it's often the simplest ideas that are the best.

Take Campbell's soup, for example. Although we might find the concept of 'condensed soup' pretty unremarkable these days, back in 1897 when it was invented by J. Dorrance it was a brilliantly simple idea, which marked the beginnings of a billion-dollar industry. Likewise, as we're on the subject of food, what on earth could be more simple than the baked beans slogan 'Beanz Meanz Heinz', or a bowl of Kellogg's Corn Flakes – which Dr Kellogg used to feed his patients in the 1890s to prevent their minds and bodies becoming too aroused?

Oh yes, without a doubt, if you're looking for that groundbreaking business idea, please don't assume that it has to be big, or complicated. It *so* doesn't have to be.

Look at Rowland Hill, for example, who revolutionised the world we live in by inventing the first adhesive postage stamp (the Penny Black) and also suggested that paying for mail could be so much more simple if it was based on weight rather than size; Lunsford Richardson, who deliberately called his vapour-rub 'Vicks' because he wanted a name that was short and easy to remember; or, perhaps to top it all, the story of the Russian scientists who avoided spending a fortune on R&D for the invention of a space pen that would work in zero-gravity conditions, by giving their cosmonauts a pencil instead!

K.I.S.S. DOODLE...

KEEP IT SO SIMPLE

TRAFFIC LIGHTS (1920)

PAPERCLIP
INVENTED BY JOHANN VAALER 1899

TESCOS
EVERY LITTLE HELPS...

COCO CHANEL'S "LITTLE BLACK DRESS" (FOR ALL OCCASIONS)

## CUNNINGLY CLEVER CREATIVITY NUGGET

Before the 1950s, if people were going to shampoo their hair they tended to do it only once and then rinse. Then the shampoo company Prell (which was owned by Procter & Gamble) had an inspired idea. 'What if we could double our sales overnight by adding just one word?' The simple word they added to 'Lather and rinse' on the back of their shampoo bottles was *repeat* and, although debate still continues as to whether this was strictly necessary for shiny healthy hair or whether it was simply a clever marketing ploy, it definitely had the desired effect of encouraging customers to use up their Prell bottles twice as quickly...

# TURNING THEORY INTO PRACTICE

**❶** Think about a current business issue you are facing and then ask yourself, 'If there was a ludicrously simple solution to this problem, what might it be?' This will provoke your mind to think beyond the usual psychological blocks of 'It's too difficult', 'It's far too complicated' or 'It can't be done'. After all, as the author John O'Keefe writes, 'We can't achieve the impossible, but we can often achieve what we *assume* to be impossible.'

**❷** What if you could simplify elements of your business – such as the design of your products, or the way you handle enquiries over the phone – to make life as 'easy' as possible for your customers? Starbucks, for example, adopted this approach when they introduced the Starbucks Card, which not only made life a little easier for customers who didn't always have the correct amount of change on them, but also led to over a 15 per cent increase in sales and revenue.

**❸** Bear in mind that 'simple' is not the same as 'simplistic', for as Edward de Bono makes clear '$E = mc^2$' might be a very simple equation, but its meaning is highly complex. Paradoxically, being simple in business is not always as simple as it looks, so be prepared for a lot of hard thinking and a lot of hard work. As the songwriter Hal David once said, 'It's easy to be simple and bad; being simple and good is quite difficult.'

---

# THINKSPIRATION
## 'Eliminate the insignificant.'
Frank Lloyd Wright (architect)

---

# LOVELY LIMITATIONS

**M**ost of us, if we're completely honest, would rather focus on our professional strengths than our weaknesses. Weaknesses are not nice. They're something to be shied away from, or brushed under the carpet, not something to be drawn attention to. Often in business, however, this approach can be a big mistake. What we think of as being our greatest weakness or limitation might actually turn out to be our greatest strength, and possibly even the best way we can differentiate ourselves from our competitors.

Take a pint of Guinness, for example. One of its **limitations** is that it takes a long time to pour. So what's great about this problem? Well, as their amazingly successful advertisements show us – like the surfer waiting for the ultimate wave – 'great things come to those who wait'.

Similarly, easyJet's major **limitation** was that they couldn't afford to give their customers all the 'frills' of an airline like British Airways. So what did they do? They used this **limitation** and offered 'no-frills' low-cost flights instead.

So, next time you're worrying about what's wrong with your business, have a go at seeing it as a plus rather than a minus. After all, would tourists bother to visit the Leaning Tower of Pisa if it was straight? Would Tommy Cooper have been such a funny comedian if he hadn't been such a lousy magician? Would the TV presenter Jonathon 'Woss' be where he is today without his famous speech impediment? Possibly not, for as Edith Piaf once said, 'Use your defects… that way you're going to be a star.'

LOVELY LIMITATIONS DOODLE...

I'M USELESS AT DRAWING, I CAN ONLY DRAW STICK PEOPLE...

LESLIE CHARTERIS AUTHOR OF "THE SAINT"

ICONIC LOGO

WHAT DO WE DO WITH THIS LEFTOVER DOUGH?

THE PRETZEL

(610 AD)

## CUNNINGLY CLEVER CREATIVITY NUGGET

J.K. Rowling's 'Harry Potter' empire has made her an even richer woman than the Queen. It could be argued, however, that the author's success might never have happened if she had not deliberately chosen to focus on the **limitations** of magic. Rowling knew from the beginning that all good stories rely on conflict, and conflict relies upon **limitations**, once saying, 'The most important thing to decide when you're creating a fantasy world is what the characters *can't* do.' So this is why even the supreme Dumbledore has a weakness such as lacking the 'power to make others see the truth'. And of course, it's why Harry Potter and his friends headed off to the wizard school 'Hogwarts' in the first place. For, let's face it, if they already knew all the answers, they'd have nothing to learn…

# TURNING THEORY INTO PRACTICE

**❶** One of the most widely used phrases in business is 'We can't afford it!' If this rings true for you, however, please don't despair or give up. Simply look at your problem through new eyes because, even with a 'limited' budget, a healthy dose of **Cunningly Clever Creativity** can often get you a long way. As Jeff Bezos (the founder of Amazon) said in an interview with *Business Week* magazine in April 2008, 'constraints drive innovation', pointing out that in the early days they had no money to spend on ad budgets but, through their 'associate programme' which linked other websites to theirs in exchange for a share of revenue, and 'one-click shopping' to help make 'check-out faster', they were able to attract many more customers.

**❷** As we all know, PR 'spin doctors' are very good at re-framing a bad experience so it's not quite so bad. But what if you could suddenly become your own corporate spin doctor? What if the next time you make a mistake you genuinely start to view it as a valuable 'learning experience'? What if, the next time you experience failure, you simply view it as an important stepping stone on the road to success? Sure, this might sound a little contrived, but it can also be immensely powerful, too. After all, it's not what happens in business that makes the difference, but what we do with what happens in business that makes the difference. That's the key.

**❸** Please bear in mind that **lovely limitations** is not about la-de-da 'positive thinking'. It's about 'focusing on the positive' of what's real.

---

## THINKSPIRATION
### 'For every disadvantage, there is a corresponding advantage.'
William Clement Stone

---

# Multiply

The **multiply** creative thinking technique is based on the question, 'What if we could do *more* of the same?' Sure, it might sound a bit obvious at first, but it's precisely this type of **Cunningly Clever Creativity** that has given us everything from the double-decker bus to the tri-plane, and cold beer six-packs to multi-storey car parks. It's also the reason why several 'Pile 'em high, sell 'em cheap' stores have become household names.

Just in case, however, examples like these lead you to assume that **multiply** is all about quantity rather than quality, please think again. Even premium brands like Tiffany, Aston Martin and The Savoy Hotel use websites to help them reach more potential customers, and this technology would not have been available if the World Wide Web's creator Tim Berners-Lee hadn't wanted to share his amazing invention with 'multiple' users.

And this is why it's important we acknowledge that **multiply** can be used in business in 'multiple' ways, from guerrilla marketing to call centres, and from the introduction of loyalty cards to the installation of new double-glazed windows. So, next time you want new solutions, keep wondering what might happen if you played 'the numbers game' and started to think less like a tiny flower shop, and more like Interflora...

## MULTIPLY DOODLE...

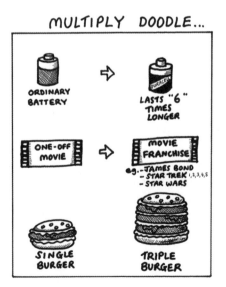

ORDINARY BATTERY ⇨ DURACELL LASTS "6" TIMES LONGER

ONE-OFF MOVIE ⇨ MOVIE FRANCHISE eg.— JAMES BOND – STAR TREK 1,2,3,4,5 – STAR WARS

SINGLE BURGER    TRIPLE BURGER

**O**ne of the best ways to boost business success is to encourage 'repeat business'. In other words, to **multiply** the number of times your customers or clients pay you for the products or services you provide... In the 1950s, on a trip to Chicago, a UK businessman called Richard Tompkins wondered why a particular garage was much busier than its competitors. When he discovered that it was because this garage handed out stamps as a reward for customers who made multiple visits (to be collected and exchanged for a variety of goods at a later date) he spotted a fantastic opportunity. He became a **clever copycat** and brought this Sperry & Hutchinson concept to the UK, calling his new business Green Shield Stamps. Within a year the stamps were already being distributed in 600 different shops and garages and, during the 1960s and 1970s, they became a huge commercial phenomenon, not just because 'multiple' people used them, but because 'multiple' people never traded them in!

## TURNING THEORY INTO PRACTICE

**❶** Have a go at brainstorming everything you associate with 'more than one' or 'more than once'. For example, a pair of shoes, a swarm of locusts, a meal in a tapas bar, a herd of buffalo, an annual subscription to a magazine, or perhaps even clocking up air miles. Then explore what you might be able to learn from each of these scenarios to help you grow your own business. For example, if you're self-employed, what if you could expand your network, so instead of always having to 'hunt' for commercial opportunities alone, you could be part of a 'pack of wolves'?

**❷** Alternatively, how about using specific numbers to help you? For example, what if you could take what you normally do in business and **multiply** it by 3, 4, 5, 6, 39 or even 101? Let each number inspire you to open your mind up to all kinds of new possibilities, in the same way that it's possible to **multiply** a unicycle to create a bicycle, a tricycle, or even a quad bike.

**❸** It could be argued that virtually every internet success story has used the **multiply** technique to some degree – from eBay to Bebo. With this in mind, imagine what you could potentially achieve if you *leveraged* the power of numbers to reach more paying customers than you ever dreamt possible...

---

## THINKSPIRATION
### 'If you want more luck, take more chances.'
Brian Tracy

---

# NUTTY NERO

The **Nutty Nero** technique is based on exaggeration. Like the mad Roman Emperor Nero himself – who was convinced he was the greatest poet and athlete to ever set foot on the planet (and would execute anyone who dared to think differently) – it involves using your mind to deliberately think in an 'over the top' way, as if you'd lost all sense of proportion.

The commercial world of entertainment, for example, is jam-packed with evidence of **Nutty Nero** at work, ranging from Superman (exaggerated strength) to the Bionic Man (exaggerated speed), and Captain America (exaggerated patriotism) to Elastigirl (exaggerated flexibility).

Elsewhere, however, there are also many other types of businesses that have prospered from using this approach, ranging from the fashion industry (just think of platform shoes!) to the food and beverage industry, which has often made heavy profits on the back of products with deliberately 'exaggerated' properties, such as the high-energy drink Red Bull, Extra Strong Mints, and the infamous Texan 'sure is a mighty chew' chocolate bar.

So, if you're looking for some innovative ideas, perhaps stop asking yourself, 'How can we make our business better?' and start asking, 'How can we make our business a *zillion* times better?'

NUTTY NERO DOODLE...

In the 1960s, Gordon Mills (the manager of an entertainer called Arnold George Dorsey) felt his artist needed a new stage persona to draw attention to himself, and help him become a big success. As a result, he considered all kinds of names, before settling on a deliberately larger than life one that nobody would forget – Englebert Humperdinck – which had been the name of a famous Austrian opera composer. As it was, the heirs of the composer sued them for this but, nevertheless, it had the desired effect of making Dorsey internationally famous.

## TURNING THEORY INTO PRACTICE

**❶** Look at an issue you are currently facing in your business (such as your marketing strategy) and then wonder what might happen if you used the **Nutty Nero** technique to fix it. Sure, you might come up with plenty of bizarre 'left-field' ideas but, at the same time, you might also stumble across a highly innovative solution like Pepsi-Cola did back in 1973 with their TV advertising slogan: 'Lipsmackin' thirstquenchin' acetastin' motivatin' goodbuzzin' cooltalkin' highwalkin' fastlivin' evergivin' coolfizzin' Pepsi.'

**❷** Many successful people in business were infamous for their exaggerating tendencies: P.T. Barnum, for example, was known as 'The King of Hyperbole' for his 'Greatest Show on Earth', and the newspaper magnate William Randolph Hearst made a fortune on the back of embellishing real stories with an almighty dose of sensationalism. So, how about you think of business exaggeration as nothing more than effective PR? This, for example, is how the founder of Granada TV, Sidney Bernstein, was able to create the impression that his production studios were far larger than they actually were, by giving the few studios he actually had even numbers (e.g. 2, 6, 8). For, let's face it, if you don't blow your own trumpet, who else will?

❸ Why not draw up a list of all the characteristics you associate with your business – such as 'reliability'or 'friendly customer service' – and then reflect on what might happen if you exaggerated like a caricaturist might with the features of someone's face? What if you were the most reliable company on earth? Or what if you provided such great customer service you even had your own 'Fan Club'?

---

## THINKSPIRATION
### 'I liked it so much I bought the company.'
Victor Kiam

---

# OUTLAW

The **outlaw** creative thinking tool involves doing what you're *not* supposed to do. It's about identifying the 'rules' and then asking yourself what might happen if you broke them, disobeyed them, or rebelled against them. Some call this approach, 'contrarian thinking' if they want to sound really clever. Others refer to it as 'outrageous opposites'.

Take, for example, the wristwatch. Back in the 1970s Swiss watches were notorious for being traditional, expensive and elitist. Unfortunately, however, although this formula had proved successful in the past, suddenly Japanese manufacturers were beginning to encroach on their market. So a forward-thinking CEO called Nicholas Hayek wondered 'what if' Swiss watches were *not* traditional, *not* expensive and *not* elitist? As a result, his company went on to develop the cool, trendy and affordable SWATCH which became the biggest-selling watch of all time.

And then, of course, let's not forget the business revolutionary of all revolutionaries – Sir Richard Branson. If people tell him, 'It can't be done', his reaction is 'Screw it, let's do it'. Once upon a time, for example, the rules were that people needed lots of different bank accounts for different reasons. Branson's team then created 'The Virgin One account'. Similarly, most major airlines felt they had to provide a First Class. Virgin was the first to ask, 'Why?'

So, next time you need a breakthrough idea, perhaps think a little more like a punk rocker or an anarchist: either rip up the rulebook or, better still, invent new rules…

OUTLAW DOODLE...

| THE "RULES" | BREAKING THE RULES |
|---|---|
| SHAPE OF CONVENTIONAL CHOCOLATE BAR | TOBLERONE |
| COMES IN JARS (HONEY) | IN A SQUEEZY BOTTLE (HONEY) |
| PANTHERS ARE BLACK | THE PINK PANTHER |

## CUNNINGLY CLEVER CREATIVITY NUGGET

Few movie stars in recent years have enjoyed the commercial success of the Asian martial artist Jackie Chan. Before Jackie Chan, Hong Kong's major martial art export had been Bruce Lee, who acted in very different types of ways, and who made very different types of films. In a magazine interview with the journalist Christopher Goodwin, Jackie Chan explained how his approach was to be the total opposite of Bruce Lee. 'If Bruce kicks high, I kick low. If he was serious, I was funny… If he is macho, I show pain and fear and avoid fights.' Chan's style definitely helped to differentiate himself from other movie stars in this genre. Another **outlaw** technique he used, was to deliberately include the 'outtakes' in his films, including the stunts that went wrong. Ironically, as Goodwin explains, 'He has become the biggest film star because of footage that *doesn't* make its way into his films!'

O

# TURNING THEORY INTO PRACTICE

**❶** Begin by drawing a vertical line down a sheet of paper, and then listing all the 'rules' of your business in the left-hand column. So, for example, if your company designs cars, the rules of cars might be: (a) They're made of metal (b) They have 4 wheels (c) They have windows to look through. Then, once you have done this, in the right-hand column systematically break each rule in the way that **outlaws** love to do. So, for example, consider what might happen if cars weren't made of metal (what if they were made of wood, flowers or rubbish?) or didn't have 4 wheels, but had 6, 3, 100, or no wheels (like a hover-car). Or, imagine if a car had no windows (like a tank), lots of windows, or was perhaps one almighty window like the Popemobile? As Edward de Bono maintains, the more closely we can identify 'what is', the easier it becomes to wonder 'what could be'.

**❷** What if your business could have the type of impact Elvis had when he first arrived on the music scene? For, as we all know, Elvis shocked many by refusing to live by the 'rules' of 1950s entertainment: for a start he was a white man who was deeply influenced by the rhythm and blues of black culture, and also his spectacular hip-wiggling – though adored by his female fans – was a step too far for many anxious parents.

**❸** Ask yourself what powerful lessons you could potentially learn from the **outlaws** of the modern business world, like Steve Jobs, who once said, 'Why join the navy when you can be a pirate?'

---

# THINKSPIRATION

## 'No one can possibly achieve any real and lasting success or "get rich" in business by being a conformist.'

John Paul Getty

---

# PERSONALISATION

There are basically two ways to use the **personalisation** technique. The first involves you deliberately 'humanising' inanimate objects, like turning an ordinary biscuit into a gingerbread man, or like Nike creating 'the intelligent shoe'. The second involves you looking at a specific problem, and then imagining that *you* are the problem, and the problem is *you*. OK, the second might sound a bit bonkers, but please don't pre-judge it too quickly because, to paraphrase Shakespeare, all too often 'there's a method in the madness'!

In the 1950s, for example, Doctor Jonas Salk developed the polio vaccine after imagining himself to be an immune system, and then visualising how he might go about fighting the virus from a human body's perspective. Similarly, Einstein came up with his theory of relativity after imagining himself to be 'personally' riding on a beam of light. This approach, however, is not solely confined to the world of scientific geniuses, for business-minded people can benefit from it, too…

The PG tips teabag, for example, allegedly owes its innovative pyramid-shaped to the **personalisation** technique. During a brainstorm, a facilitator asked the question, 'How would you feel if *you* were a teabag in a teapot?' To which someone replied, 'Squashed' and 'I'd want to be able to breathe.' As a result, they went on to create a radically different type of bag, which not only gave tea more space to breathe, but also helped PG to differentiate itself from its many competitors…

PERSONALISATION DOODLE...

" THE SPEAKING CLOCK " (1937)

THOMAS THE TANK ENGINE (Rev. W.V. AWDRY: 1946)

## CUNNINGLY CLEVER CREATIVITY NUGGET

The former Synectics innovation consultant Jonne Ceserani tells a story of some people in the USA who loved to go clay-pigeon shooting but faced a big problem. Every time one of their members shot a clay pigeon it would break up into lots of different pieces, and the fragments would end up falling on people's lawns. With good reason, those living in the local community were getting increasingly fed up, and wanted the place closed down. So one day the clay-pigeon shooters had a brainstorm in which the facilitator said, 'OK, how might you feel if *you* were the clay pigeon, and you landed on people's lawns?' As you might expect, there were the predictable 'shattered' and 'smashed' remarks. However, when asked again, 'How would you really, really feel?', someone said, 'Embarrassed. I'd want to melt away.'

This led to someone else saying, 'Hey, ice melts. What if we made the clay pigeons out of ice instead?' and then a further member of the group added, 'What if we could add nutrients to the ice, too, so next time the pieces land on people's lawns they not only water the grass, but also fertilise the soil, too?'…

## TURNING THEORY INTO PRACTICE

**1** If you face a particular business challenge right now – such as cashflow – take a moment to consider how you might feel if *you* were the cashflow and the cashflow was *you*? For example, would you be flowing as smoothly as a gentle stream, or as wildly and recklessly as a raging torrent? Is there a way of you increasing your flow by adding new revenue streams, or perhaps even slowing down your flow by building the financial equivalent of a dam?

**❷** What if you could look at the most mechanistic parts of your business – such as boring old admin – and then ask yourself in what ways you could help to bring them to life by making them more human or people-centric?

**❸** How about using **personalisation** next time you need to influence someone who's causing you a problem at work, by truly imagining that you are them, and they are you. 'Walk a mile in their moccasins', as the cliché goes, because – clutzy as it might sound – often people won't care what we know until they know we care...

---

## THINKSPIRATION
### 'You have to have your heart in the business, and the business in your heart.'
Thomas J. Watson (founder of IBM)

---

# QUICK-SLOW

The **quick-slow** creative thinking technique focuses on 'tempo', inviting you to wonder what might happen if you started to speed things up or slow things down in a business context.

Domino Pizzas, for example, experienced a huge boost in sales when they offered their 'delivery in 30 minutes or your money back' guarantee. Similarly, the UK car-exhaust firm Kwik-Fit's original advertising campaign, 'You can't get quicker than a Kwik-Fit fitter', helped to turn its founder, Sir Tom Farmer, into a billionaire.

Making things faster, however, isn't always the answer. In fact, sometimes the complete opposite is true. A parachute, for example, is useful because it slows down a person's descent. Similarly, escalators in shops are meant to be slow, giving customers the time to look around to see what else is on offer. It's also why supermarkets deliberately put day-to-day essentials like bread and milk at the back of their stores, to 'slow' down customers who might normally rush in and out and to tempt them into buying additional goods.

So, how about using the **quick-slow** technique to play around with time? After all, time is without doubt our most precious resource...

QUICK-SLOW DOODLE...

FAST COFFEE...
ESPRESSO
(ESPRESSO MACHINE INVENTED BY ACHILLE GAGGIA: 1938)

BOOK TRAVEL ARRANGEMENTS A LONG TIME IN ADVANCE → Lastminute.com

EATING SWEETS QUICKLY... → MURRAY MINTS... "TOO GOOD TO HURRY MINTS" (AD CAMPAIGN)

I n 1917 a scientist on a hunting expedition to Labrador, Canada, noticed how the local fish tasted remarkably fresh, even though it had been frozen, compared to the mushy stuff he was used to back home, which was full of ice crystals. He soon realised that this was because the fish was instantly frozen the moment it was taken out of the water and thrown onto the ice. In other words, the process was a 'quick' one, rather than a slow one. As a result, the scientist – Captain Birdseye – went on to invent a clever way of replicating this 'fast-freezing' effect, and create a massive new industry of which fish fingers are … dare I say it… simply the tip of the iceberg.

## TURNING THEORY INTO PRACTICE

**1** Is there a part of your business that is perhaps attempting to move too fast? Do you always feel in such a rush that your performance is getting worse rather than better? If so, how about reflecting on what might happen if you deliberately slowed things down a little. When the typewriter was first invented in 1868, for example, secretaries became so proficient at using them that the machines used to jam up when working at such a speed. As a result, a man called James Densmore – who was an associate of its inventor Sholes – suggested the QWERTY system – which we still use today – which prevents the most frequently used keys being clustered together.

**2** Many of us procrastinate at work, whether we like to admit it or not. Sometimes, we even justify this to ourselves with excuses like, 'I don't have the time' or 'It will take too long'. If this is true for you, how about using the **quick-slow** technique to challenge these mental assumptions? For example, if you write for a living, why not 'create an emergency' to speed things up a bit, and reflect on how, if *The Bridges of Madison County* only took 3 weeks to write and *The Day of the Jackal* only took 35 days, what's taking you so long?

**❸** If you genuinely value the service you provide for your customers, never stop asking yourself **quick-slow** questions such as, 'What if we could allow our customers to relax more by providing a service that sways like a hammock, and is as slow as a sunset?' or 'What if we could meet their needs twice as fast, or ten times faster?'

---

## THINKSPIRATION
### 'The world is changing very fast. Big will not beat small any more. It will be the fast beating the slow.'
Rupert Murdoch

---

# REDUCE

How many of us, from an early age, are taught to believe that big = better? Well, weirdly enough, in business it often turns out that the opposite is true. Big means cumbersome. Big means bulky. Big means slow. Small, on the other hand, can boost all kinds of benefits.

The **reduce** creative thinking tool enables us to wonder what might happen if we could wave a magic wand and 'shrink' whatever's in front of us, rather like the movie *Honey, I Shrunk the Kids*.

Obvious examples that might spring to mind include miniature versions of existing products, such as the iPod nano, or 'small-screen TV'. It can also, however, include anything 'bite-size', ranging from chocolate biscuits to management training courses, or 'pint-size', such as the clothes retailer Gap (for kids).

In this respect, it would be easy to provide you with a very long list of examples, from keyhole surgery to Tom Thumb, but that, of course, would be defeating the whole point of this technique. So, let's keep it short and snappy, and end with a highly successful strapline Volkswagen once used in an ad campaign…

Think Small.

## CUNNINGLY CLEVER CREATIVITY NUGGET

Historically, many of the poorest people in Bangladesh were unable to get a bank loan of any description because they were simply unable to provide the security banks were looking for. Then, in 1973, a man called Muhammad Yunus decided to set up a new type of banking system to get around this problem, which became known as 'micro-financing'. As a result, not only does the Grameen Bank now have 2,442 branches but, because of his **Cunningly Clever Creativity** and social entrepreneurship, Yunus ended up winning the 2006 Nobel Peace Prize. Not bad, really, for a little idea…

## TURNING THEORY INTO PRACTICE

**❶** What if you could wave a magic wand like Merlin and deliberately 'shrink' parts of your business, such as a product, service, or perhaps even the length of most meetings? Playing around with scale – rather like Jonathan Swift did in *Gulliver's Travels* – can often lead to a wide range of innovative ideas.

**❷** Think of all the words you tend to associate with 'reduction', and then see what happens when you start to combine them with specific aspects of your business. For example, consider words like 'nano', 'compact', 'mini', 'bite-size', 'taster', 'sample' and 'nutshell'…

❸ How about finding inspiration by looking at other companies that have used the **reduce** technique to boost business success, such as Toyota with its 'lean manufacturing' or certain hand-held products like the PalmPilot? And then, as always, apply back what you have learnt or discovered to your own unique situation:

REDUCE REDUCE REDUCE REDUCE REDUCE....

---

## THINKSPIRATION
### 'The little things in life are infinitely the most important.'
Sir Arthur Conan Doyle

---

# SWAPSHOP

If you want to generate new ideas in a hurry, you might fancy giving **swapshop** a go. All you have to do is look at a specific part of your business (or perhaps even several parts of it) and ask yourself, 'What if I substituted *this* for *that*?', rather like swapping analogue technology for digital technology, waitress-service for self-service, or eco-nasty plastic containers for biodegradable containers.

Take the chocolate manufacturer Mars, for example. Mars realised that in the heat of the summer people usually eat less chocolate and more ice cream, causing sales to fall. So what did they do? They came up with the idea of swapping the inside of a conventional Mars bar for ice cream, creating the 'Mars Ice Cream Bar'.

Or how about the inventor Trevor Bayliss, whose amazing 'clockwork radio' involved substituting traditional alkaline batteries for a 'wind-up' device instead, making it far easier and cheaper for many of the poorest communities in Africa to finally receive radio communication?

And then, of course, looking at the bigger picture, it could be argued that the whole of human progress has always involved 'swapping' one thing for another anyway – from the candle to the gaslight and the gaslight to the light bulb – so keep this in mind if you want to move your business on. Exit the old, enter the new…

## SWAPSHOP DOODLE...

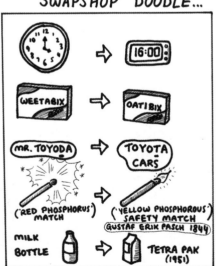

# CUNNINGLY CLEVER CREATIVITY NUGGET

One of the most successful commercial songwriters of the last 25 years – Dianne Warren – has often used **swapshop** to create memorable song titles (although 'The Paragram Technique' is its official term if you want to sound really clever). The way it works is you take a well-known phrase and then deliberately replace one word with another. So, this is how she managed to turn 'Where Do I Go From *Here*?' into 'Where Do I Go From *You*?', '*Faith* Can Move Mountains' into '*Love* Can Move Mountains', and '*Don't* Break My Heart' into '*Un*break My Heart'. In fact, you may have noticed this type of creativity also being used in the world of eye-catching newspaper headlines. During the Falkands War, for example, the UK tabloid *The Sun* turned the phrase 'Stick it up your jumper' into 'Stick it up your junta'… Mmm… well… with that said, let's move swiftly on…

## TURNING THEORY INTO PRACTICE

**❶** Please take a long hard look at the different 'component parts' of your business and then reflect on what might happen if you zapped them with **swapshop**. It could be one part or two, several or all. Whatever. The trick here is to hold nothing 'sacred'. Anything goes… literally. For example, you might want to consider **swapping** an existing element that's large for one that's small, but why stop there? **Swap** old for new, linear for circular, wooden for metal, red for blue, blunt for sharp, hot for cold, expensive for cheap, sensible for wild, and so on… the possibilities are endless.

**②** Alternatively, how about focusing on **swapping** 'words' to help you become more innovative with your branding, marketing, report writing or internal communications? For example, maybe have a go at turning words into letters – rather like the rock band INXS (in excess) or the pop band XTC (ecstasy) – or even parts of words for other words, as the sunglasses brand Police recently did with their strapline 'YOUnique'. Or maybe **swap** the 'way' you talk to others?

**③** Think of **swapshop** rather like a football manager substituting one player for another, and consider what a difference it can often make (to the team and the result) to replace someone tired with someone fresh and full of energy. Perhaps think about 'who' you could **swap**, rather than 'what', to make a positive change to your business...

---

## THINKSPIRATION
### 'Don't be afraid to give up the good to go for the great.'
John D. Rockefeller

---

# TRANSFER

The **transfer** technique involves taking what works (or perhaps doesn't work) in one context, and then applying it to another.

Look at Viagra, for example. It was originally intended to be a drug for people suffering from angina, before its developers soon realised it had a rather unexpected side effect! Similarly, the jacuzzi was originally intended for use in agriculture to help churn up the soil, but it subsequently became better known for the way it produces bubbles in luxury bathrooms. Or what about genetic fingerprinting – the brainchild of Alec Jeffreys – which was originally intended for helping people to explore their heritage, before police forensics quickly snapped it up to help solve over a million crimes!

Yes, it may be true that lots of **transfer** successes are simply random events, like the Frisbee (which was the result of its inventor throwing an empty Frisbie pie tin and being amazed at how well it could fly). But not all are. **Transfer** can also be a highly effective mindtool for provoking fresh questions like, 'What else can we do with this, to make money?' That's why it's no coincidence that NASA has a division known as The NASA Knowledge Transfer Unit which focuses on **transferring** space technology breakthroughs into the commercial sector, inspiring all kinds of innovations, from new sunglasses to bedroom mattresses. There's even a book called *Ideas from Outer Space*, based on their work, which says it all, really…

## TRANSFER DOODLE...

| FROM HERE... | TO THERE... |
|---|---|
| BALLPOINT PEN | ROLL-ON DEODORANT |
| "PRUTEEN" (ORIGINALLY USED AS ANIMAL FEED) | QUORN |
| OIL / PETROLEUM JELLY | VASELINE |

## CUNNINGLY CLEVER CREATIVITY NUGGET

Entrepreneurs are often very good at using the **transfer** technique, instinctively seeing how something in one context might have commercial potential in another. Take the toy-football game Subbuteo, for example. It was originally created by a man called Peter Adolph in 1947 who noticed that there was a huge surplus of green fabric left over after World War II. Asking the question, 'What can be done with all this material?' the solution he came up with was to convert it into mini-football pitches, initially encouraging purchasers to 'Mark your pitch on an ex-Army blanket'. In the years that followed, he went on to manufacture pre-made football pitches and a range of other accessories, which helped to successfully **transfer** him into a multi-millionaire...

# TURNING THEORY INTO PRACTICE

**1** If you work in a business that makes a particular product, how about asking yourself, 'What else could we use this product for?', 'What if we could apply the same underlying principles that work here to a totally new context?' or 'What if we could branch out, and start selling our product to a different generation, a different gender, or perhaps in parts of the world we've never even considered before?'

**2** Alternatively, instead of thinking of 'products' maybe focus on 'services', 'skills' or 'personality'. How might you be able to take what you do, or who you are, and **transfer** it so you can add value to an alternative or additional marketplace?

After all, this is how the comedian John Cleese made £9 million when he sold Video Arts, the sales training company he originally set up to make boring corporate videos more humorous and entertaining. It's also how Paul Newman – the Hollywood heart-throb – successfully managed to **transfer** his film-star status onto the labels of pasta sauce jars with his famous brand Newman's Own, which to date has donated over $200 million to a range of charities...

**3** It is often said that 'One man's rubbish, is another man's gold.' Might there be anything in your business which you perceive as 'worthless', but others might view as valuable? Storage? Advice? Contacts?...

---

# THINKSPIRATION
**'Creativity is not the finding of a thing, but the making something out of it after it is found.'**
James Russell Lowell

---

# U-TURN

The **U-turn** creative thinking technique involves going backwards instead of forwards to find winning business ideas. It's all about realising that sometimes turning the clock back is, rather strangely, one of the most innovative things we can do.

Take the fashion outlet Laura Ashley, for example. During the 1970s her floral prints and milkmaid clothes were a million miles from trendy, but somehow they still managed to sell like hot cakes to mothers and daughters who found comfort in her 'brand new version of the past'.

Similarly, the best-selling manual *The Dangerous Book for Boys* became a commercial publishing phenomenon in 2006 not so much because it was radically 'new', but because – in a digital world of computer games and mobile phones – its helpful lessons on tying knots and building tree-houses were refreshingly 'old'.

So, if you're looking for a healthy dose of inspiration, don't always assume that the future holds the key, because, as they say, 'There is nothing new under the sun...'

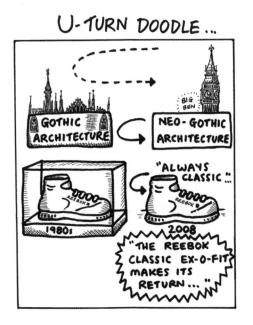

U-TURN DOODLE...

GOTHIC ARCHITECTURE

NEO-GOTHIC ARCHITECTURE

BIG BEN

"ALWAYS CLASSIC..."

1980s

2008

REEBOK

"THE REEBOK CLASSIC EX-O-FIT MAKES ITS RETURN..."

## CUNNINGLY CLEVER CREATIVITY NUGGET

Ted Turner is known the world over for having created the 24-hour news channel CNN – the Cable News Network – back in 1980. This enterprise, however, was by no means the first or last of his clever business ideas. A decade earlier he had bought a television channel in Atlanta called Channel 17, which had dreadful ratings and minimal advertising revenue. And what did he do with it? Fill it with highly innovative and original TV shows as you might expect? No. On the contrary. Using a **U-turn** mindset he simply decided to give the viewing public reruns and nothing but reruns. He gave them classic old black and white movie after classic old black and white movie, and the result was a resounding success.

## TURNING THEORY INTO PRACTICE

**❶** What if you could use ideas from the past to give you ideas for the future? For example, if your business is hit by a recession, how about doing some research on how other businesses managed to survive and thrive the last recession, or perhaps even the Great Depression of the 1920s and 30s? Yes, the circumstances might be different, but some of the underlying principles might still be the same...

**❷** Some businesses make the mistake of over-diversifying. Along the way they forget who they really are, and lose their core purpose. If this is true for you, how about casting your mind back to the early days, and asking yourself, 'What if we could get back to basics, and from now on only focus on what we're really, really good at?'

**❸** The word inspiration comes from the Latin *in spirare* meaning 'to breathe into'. What if you could breathe new life into the more traditional or antiquated parts of your business? If you do, you just might find that, like Aladdin, the rusty old lamp you're rubbing and polishing is not so worthless after all. One recent example of this approach is the UK supermarket Sainsbury's, which has been losing a lot of its market share to rivals like Tesco and Asda. In 2007 its CEO Justin King felt it was time to 'restore London's oldest grocer to its former position', re-introducing bags for life based on designs dating back 127 years, to help boost brand loyalty. As he put it in an article in *The Times*, 'We're reaching back to be better in the future. We're not doing this just for nostalgia.'

---

## THINKSPIRATION
### 'Nothing is as new as something which has been long forgotten.'
German Proverb

---

# VARIATIONS

The **variations** technique is ultimately a 'tweaking' tool which helps us to make minor alterations to what's gone before. Unlike most of the other mindtools in this book, it's not really interested in radical change or creativity with a big C. Quite the opposite. It's far more interested in incremental change, and creativity with a small c...

Take Ribena, for example. For years this fruit-drink manufacturer focused on making blackcurrant drinks, and nothing but blackcurrant drinks. In fact, one year it allegedly bought up 100 per cent of the UK blackcurrant crop! More recently, however, it has decided to branch out into making other types of fruit drinks, too, such as cranberry and blackcurrant, blueberry and even raspberry and pomegranate. Now admittedly this might not be earth-shatteringly innovative, but who cares? Sometimes tiny innovations can make a world of difference, and they can also be a lot less risky, too.

Similarly, consider Radox, which has been helping people to relax for over 100 years with the famous green pine-smelling bubble bath. Recently, however, its manufacturer too has decided to offer customers a broader range of alternatives to the original juniper formula, including Moisture Soak (a pink mixture containing calendula), Time Out (a purple mixture containing mimosa) and Sleep Easy (a bluish formula containing lavender).

So, why not have a go at making minor alterations to your business? All you have to do is play around with the 'same but different' concept, and see what happens...

# VARIATIONS DOODLE...

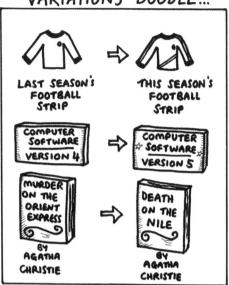

LAST SEASON'S FOOTBALL STRIP ⇨ THIS SEASON'S FOOTBALL STRIP

COMPUTER SOFTWARE VERSION 4 ⇨ COMPUTER SOFTWARE VERSION 5

MURDER ON THE ORIENT EXPRESS BY AGATHA CHRISTIE ⇨ DEATH ON THE NILE BY AGATHA CHRISTIE

## CUNNINGLY CLEVER CREATIVITY NUGGET

James Bond is one of the most successful movie franchises in history. But although each film is different – from *Diamonds are Forever* to *Casino Royale* and *Live and Let Die* to *Goldeneye* – deep down they're basically all **variations** on the same theme. As Bond's creator Ian Fleming once said, they're all about 'Kiss kiss, bang bang': an evil megalomaniac tries to take over the world, and only one man – the suave super-spy James Bond – is able to stop him, which he always successfully manages to do against incredible odds whilst gallivanting around a vast array of exotic locations, driving fast cars, playing around with fancy weaponry, and sleeping with beautiful women. Fleming knew that if you're lucky enough to stumble upon a winning formula which people love, want more of, and are prepared to pay for, you'd be a fool to change it. Or at least, to change it *too* much.

# TURNING THEORY INTO PRACTICE

**1** How about asking yourself the question, 'What if we could change what we do, but only slightly?' Hopefully you'll find this a fairly easy exercise but, if you don't, you might want to draw inspiration from **variations** in other walks of life. Take, 'hats', for example. A hat is simply something you wear on your head. But just think of how many **variations** of hats there are in the world, from top hats to baseball caps, and lace bonnets to military berets. Or how about 'bread'? Bread's simply a food made out of milled grain. But again, just think of its countless **variations**, from brown loaves to white rolls, and French croissants to peshwari naan.

**2** Why not have a go at using the **variations** tool in conjunction with other tools in this book to help generate fresh ideas? For example, use it with **reduce** to make something just a little bit smaller, or with **enlarge** to make something just a little bit bigger, or with **quick-slow** to make something just a little bit faster or slower?

**3** It is often said that 'attitude is altitude'. What if you could use **variations** to help bring about a tiny shift in either your own attitude, or the attitude of those you work with? Imagine how much more could potentially be achieved.

---

# THINKSPIRATION
## 'Many "big" improvements are the results of many "small" improvements.'
W. Edward Deming

---

# WOBBLE

The **wobble** technique is based on identifying what it is that **wobbles** people, and then turning those *fears into ideas*. It's often effective because deep down we're all afraid of something (even Napoleon was afraid of cats!). So, if a clever entrepreneur or inventor can come along with a solution for minimising or eliminating that fear, then bingo! **Wobbled** people will probably be only too happy to pay for it. And this, of course, is why we live in a world that's chock-a-block with everything from burglar alarms to pet insurance, and safety pins to organic food and vitamin tablets.

Oddly enough, however, this technique can also work the opposite way by deliberately choosing to give people **wobbles**, rather than take them away. Think of Alfred Hitchcock, the movie director, for example, who made his fortune on the back of suspense thrillers. Or, come to mention it, every other form of **wobble** entertainment, from horror films to ghost trains, and also the entire 'adrenaline junkie' industry with its bungee jumping, cloud surfing, and diving in shark-infested waters.

Wooooooooh yes. The fact is that 'fear' is an incredibly powerful emotion and also a highly effective influencing tool, too. So, if you want new ideas to help boost your business success, don't be afraid to use it…

## WOBBLE DOODLE…

FEAR OF …

| LOOKING OLDER | → | ANTI-WRINKLE CREAM |

| NOT HEARING "BABY" WHEN THEY NEED HELP | → | BABY MONITOR |

| DRINKING "IMPURE" TAP WATER | → | WATER FILTER |

## CUNNINGLY CLEVER CREATIVITY NUGGET

One of the biggest **wobbles** on the planet has to be anxious parents worrying about the safety of their kids. This is a major reason why Volvo – the Swedish car company founded in 1927 – has managed to be so successful, because instead of trying to build really fast cars, or flash cars, it has gone out of its way to build solid and reliable cars which family-minded adults find strong and secure. Over the years this **wobble** focus has inspired them to come up with a multitude of accident protection innovations ranging from three-point safety belts to rear-facing child seats and crumple zones to side-collision protection, helping them to stay relevant in a fiercely competitive marketplace.

## TURNING THEORY INTO PRACTICE

**❶** As a manager, you might find it helpful to create a **Wobble List** of anything and everything you can think of that **wobbles** your competition, customers and staff. You can then use this list to start triggering new ideas.

For example, supposing one of the **wobbles** you write down is how certain members of your team feel stressed and uncertain about the future, and this is having a negative effect on their performance. What if you could use this information as a catalyst to help improve the way you communicate authentically with them, so they end up with a much clearer picture of where they stand and of the positive contribution you would love them to make going forwards?

**❷** Without turning yourself into a 'New Machiavelli', how about at least brainstorming the commercial value of exploiting people's fears? Remember the so-called Millennium Bug (or Y2K bug), for example, where everyone thought that computers would go do-lally come 1 January 2000? Nothing ever happened. But this still didn't stop a lot of management consultants and IT experts making millions for overstating the emergency and providing paranoid executives with well-needed peace of mind.

❸ It is often said that 'fear' holds us back more than anything else in life: the fear of failure, fear of success, fear of humiliation, fear of rejection, fear of making mistakes, and so the list goes on. Perhaps take a moment or two to explore your own fears, and what it is that **wobbles** you on a personal level. Why? Because the sooner we can appreciate that fear is simply a natural emotion that's encouraging us to 'be prepared' – or to put it another way 'friendly energy announcing risk' – we can then begin to use it in a positive way, and turn our stumbling blocks into stepping stones.

---

## THINKSPIRATION
## 'Fear is the biggest motivator.'
Bill Dixon

---

# X-RAY

The **X-ray** technique involves looking 'under the skin' of business, to see what others fail to see. Like Sherlock Holmes – who once turned to Watson and said, 'You see but you do not observe' – it's a deeply insightful approach which is why (of all the tools in this book) it's also probably the most 'clever'.

Obviously, many entrepreneurs over the years have used it instinctively, such as Sidney Bernstein – the founder of Granada TV – who we mentioned earlier. Back in the 1950s when other UK TV companies were competing to win franchises, most focused on those areas of the country with the greatest density of population to get the highest TV audiences. But not Bernstein. He used **X-ray** to go beneath and beyond this way of thinking. He focused his attention on the area with the highest annual rainfall, which turned out to be near Manchester, realising that 'More rain = more people staying at home watching TV'.

Similarly, innovation consultant Michael Michalko talks about the new CEO of a pen company who asked his colleagues, 'What do we do here?' 'We make pens,' they said, slightly alarmed that he didn't know. But the new CEO was looking beneath the surface. 'And what do people buy those pens for?' 'Usually as gifts,' was the answer. 'Ah,' he then said. 'So we're in the gift business,' and with this simple paradigm shift they were able to revise their strategic direction, and radically boost the profit margin of the company.

As these examples show, if you're on the quest for breakthrough business ideas and solutions, please don't settle for the obvious because, as Sherlock Holmes also once said, 'Nothing is as deceptive as an obvious fact.' Put on your imaginary **X-ray** specs and ask yourself, 'What's *really* going on here?' And, if you're not sure, look again, only deeper…

# X-RAY DOODLE...

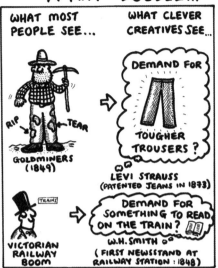

WHAT MOST PEOPLE SEE...

WHAT CLEVER CREATIVES SEE...

RIP — TEAR

GOLDMINERS (1849)

DEMAND FOR TOUGHER TROUSERS?

LEVI STRAUSS (PATENTED JEANS IN 1873)

TRAINS

VICTORIAN RAILWAY BOOM

DEMAND FOR SOMETHING TO READ ON THE TRAIN?

W.H. SMITH (FIRST NEWSSTAND AT RAILWAY STATION : 1848)

## CUNNINGLY CLEVER CREATIVITY NUGGET

**B**ack in the late 1990s, **X-ray** thinkers Sergey Brin and Larry Page noticed something about search engines on the internet that many others failed to realise: 'Not all pages are created equal, some are more important than others.' As a result, they went on to develop the PageRank algorithm (whatever that is), making the process of searching for information much speedier and more relevant to people's enquiries, attracting more and more customers, and also businesses who were happy to pay for 'the inclusion of small, highly targeted text advertisements that searchers click on for information'. According to author David Vise in his book *The Google Story*, few spotted the commercial possibilities of Google at the time, including companies like AltaVista who could have bought it for $1 million while Brin and Page were still students at Stanford University: 'By the summer of 2005, each of the founders had a net worth of more than $10 billion.'

# TURNING THEORY INTO PRACTICE

**1** In psychology, a 'schotoma' is the fancy word given to what happens when we literally can't see something, even though it's staring us in the face. Could it be that the business solution you're looking for is so obvious you keep missing it, like the glasses on the end of your nose? How about you stopped looking in faraway places for business solutions, and started looking much closer to home?

**2** As we all know, one of the major reasons companies bring in external management consultants is to get an 'outside eye' on their business issues. What if you could be your own management consultant for the day, week or month, and apply a similar level of scrutiny? Who knows? You might end up getting to the root of your problems much faster, and for only a fraction of the cost.

**3** In the world of medicine, **X-rays** can often help to spot a potential problem before it becomes a real problem. What if you could apply a similar 'prevention is better than cure' mindset to your own business? Edward de Bono, for example, is often a strong advocate of the 'problem avoidance' use of creativity, saying, 'Instead of solving the problem you go upstream and alter the system so the problem does not occur in the first place.'

# THINKSPIRATION
## 'All my life I've looked at words as if seeing them for the first time.'
Ernest Hemingway

# YOGURT

In the same way that **yogurt** is often used to put 'good bacteria' back into our bodies, the **yogurt** creative thinking technique is all about using our minds to switch direction, and to spin things around. Some like to call it 'reversal'; others prefer to call it 'upside-down' thinking. The underlying principles, however, are much the same.

Take, for example, Henry Ford's creation of the production line for the automobile industry. Instead of the workers going to the cars, he asked the question, 'What if the cars went to the workers?'

Similarly, a man called Mike Cullen used the **yogurt** approach to invent the supermarket back in the 1920s. Traditionally, people used to go into shops, tell the shopkeeper what they wanted to buy, and then the shopkeeper would fetch it for them before they paid for it. Cullen wondered, 'What might happen if we twisted this around so, instead of the shopkeepers bringing the goods to the customers, the customers brought the goods to the shopkeepers?'

So 'reverse' away to your heart's content if you want to generate new ideas for business success, for this is how Mandy Haberman invented the children's non-spillable drinking beaker the Anywayup Cup, and Trebor mints derived its name from the word Robert...

# YOGURT DOODLE...

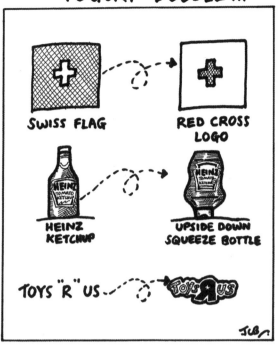

SWISS FLAG → RED CROSS LOGO

HEINZ KETCHUP → UPSIDE DOWN SQUEEZE BOTTLE

TOYS "R" US →

JLB

## CUNNINGLY CLEVER CREATIVITY NUGGET

One of the most commercially successful comedians of recent years is Ricky Gervais (best known for his TV hit *The Office*). Together with his co-writer, it appears that he used the **yogurt** technique for his other major commercial smash, *Extras*. Normally in TV and film, 'extras' are the actors who linger in the background, whom people fail to notice. Gervais, however, reversed this concept, making the ordinary people with the fewest lines become the lead characters, and the big named leading characters take a back seat with only cameo roles.

# TURNING THEORY INTO PRACTICE

**❶** Take a good look at your existing business (in terms of your systems, structures, processes and procedures) and then consider what might happen if you reversed the normal direction specific parts flow in. For example, what if instead of A moving to B, B moved to A? Or what if W could be reversed into M, or M into W? Supermarkets have done precisely this in recent years by providing home delivery for internet shoppers, reversing the concept of 'shop until you drop' into 'you shop, we'll drop'. Wackier still, the very innovative Brazilian company Semco has created a system where the workers hire and fire managers rather than the managers hiring and firing the workers (mmm… not too sure about that one).

**❷** If you are an entrepreneur who is looking for a new name for your company, you could do worse than experiment with the **yogurt** technique: Oprah Winfrey, for example, used it to create her production company Harpo Productions; Sir Bob Geldof used it to create Ten Alps as a new venture following the success of his other company, Planet 24.

**❸** Another approach to **yogurt** can be to use 'outside-in' or 'inside-out' thinking. For example, Disney makes a children's dress which is a brown Cinderella outfit if worn one way (i.e. rags) but, when turned inside out, it becomes a beautiful light blue Cinders ball gown. What if you could adapt this concept to your own business? What extra possibilities, for example, might there be relating to outsourcing, or reverse engineering? Or what if, instead of external consultants coming to help you, you could exploit your expertise and act as a consultant to others?

---

# THINKSPIRATION
**'Management is about applying human skills to systems, not applying systems to people.'**
Henry Mintzberg

---

# ZEBRA

The **zebra** creative thinking technique involves asking yourself what might happen if you deliberately 'divided' something up into different parts (much like the black and white stripes of a zebra). It's basically all about segmentation and separation.

Yes, this might sound a bit wacky to begin with, but consider the university student Alex Tew, who set up **www.milliondollarpage .com**. What did he do? He simply set up a single page on the internet, divided it up into a million pixels, and then he sold each pixel for $1 as a means of generating advertising revenue. Not a bad way to pay off a student loan, don't you think?

Another example, of course, includes the pioneering work of the economist Adam Smith, who suggested in the *Wealth of Nations* (1776) that organisations could boost their productivity by encouraging different people to specialise on different tasks – in what became known as 'the division of labour'.

So, next time you visit a warehouse which has been divided up into self-storage units, or even open up a lever-arch file which is full of multi-coloured 'divider cards', please take a moment to reflect on how powerful **zebra** can be for boosting business success. Let's face it, without Adam Smith, business as we know it might not exist at all...

ZEBRA DOODLE...

BOX

PILL BOX

**B**ack in 1815, many miners used to die in explosions caused when a candle flame reacted with escaped methane gas. The engineer Sir Humphry Davy (1778–1829) wondered what might happen if he could separate the one from the other. The end result was that he invented the 'Davy lamp' which managed to keep the flame and the gas apart, and this **zebra** division is estimated to have saved thousands of lives…

# TURNING THEORY INTO PRACTICE

**❶** What do you currently do in business that could potentially be improved by slicing it up into smaller units? Project management? Product design? Office layout? How about seeing 'solid' entities rather like a piece of cake, which you could possibly cut in half, divide into quarters, or perhaps even into eight equal parts… Then ask yourself what might happen if you could start to divide it from the side, as well as from the top.

**❷** Instead of focusing purely on units of 'space', how about taking a closer look at units of 'time'. Ask yourself in what ways could you potentially carve up your working day to achieve more, from a time management perspective? Or, if you are managing an organisation, in what ways could you use **zebra** to improve the working conditions and performance of your team, such as the introduction of more flexi-time and a better work–life balance?

**❸** Let your mind dwell on the word 'divide' for a little while, and then apply back your new ideas to your own unique situation. For example, if you are finding it hard to control your team, perhaps consider the advantages of divide and rule; if your organisation is suffering from a range of conflict management issues, ask yourself what lessons you could potentially learn from the way Moses parted the Red Sea; or, if you feel overwhelmed by too many day-to-day working commitments, picture how a deli owner is able to change the settings on a slicing machine, to sometimes cut thick slices of ham, and at other times to cut very thin slices of salami. (Of course, if you are a vegetarian, you might want to change this image to a carpenter or paper-maker chopping up wood).

## THINKSPIRATION
**'Nothing is particularly hard if you divide it into smaller jobs.'**
Henry Ford

**Z**

# AND FINALLY...

Before we leave the subject of idea generation, a pretty important point.

Please don't think that you have to use 'one' tool in isolation at all times.

You don't.

There may be occasions when you'd prefer to mix and match different tools together to stimulate fresh ideas.

For example, there is a highly successful self-storage company in the UK called The Big Yellow which appears to have blended **enlarge** with **zebra** and **outlaw**, turning traditionally drab and dreary storage buildings into brightly coloured ones, and replacing conventional brick-wall divisions with metal screens.

Alternatively, if you're in the mood, have a good look at the **Genius** childrens' book *Alice in Wonderland*. Throughout it you'll find all kinds of **Cunningly Clever Creativity Tools** being used, from **reduce** to **Nutty Nero** and **personalisation** to **swapshop**. And, yes, it might be an incredibly odd literary masterpiece, but who can dispute its commercial success?

So, by all means, feel free to 'Pick & Mix' to your heart's content, especially if it's **Genius Moments** you're after...

# IDEAS INTO ACTION

'If you have built your castles in the air, your work need not be lost; that is where they should be. Now put the foundations under them.'

Henry David Thoreau

**OK,** now you've had a chance to explore 26 different mindtools for helping you to generate new business ideas and hopefully you've come up with a long list of possibilities. What next?

Here's an easy 4-step plan to help you select and refine them.

## THE 4 C's

→ Choose

→ Check

→ Cycle

→ Climb

## 1 CHOOSE

Take a good look at your super-duper list of ideas, and then choose *one* you're keen to develop. That's right, not 10 or 20, just 1 for now because you can always come back later to choose more, if need be.

As you do so, however, please base your decision on what the company Synectics call 'intrigue'. An idea that has something fresh about it. An idea that makes you curious. An idea that whets your imagination, so you want to dig a little deeper, and find out more…

In other words, don't just pick an idea because you like it or don't like it, because you think it'll be easy to implement or will possibly make you a quick buck. If you make your selection like that, you'll probably end up in 'run-of-the-mill' territory, with an idea that's pretty dull, familiar and predictable.

Instead, choose an idea that is 'spikey' rather than safe.

By the way, if you're facilitating a group brainstorm, the principle's much the same, but you'll need to make sure in advance what type of 'selection' criteria you're going to be using.

For example, are you going to be giving everyone in the room an equal vote, or are you going to 'weight' it, depending on rank or seniority? Are you going to let everyone decide or, ultimately, let one person decide – usually the boss whose neck is on the line if it all goes wrong?

If it's a group vote you're after, here are two techniques that can help:

→ *Funny money:* Give everyone in the room an imaginary £100, and then ask them to spend it in whatever way they'd like, based on their own personal ratings of the ideas available. For example, one person might give £50 to one idea, and then £50 to another, or another person might give £70 to the first, £20 to the second, and £10 to the third. At the end, the scores are added up, and the idea (or ideas) with the most money attached to it (or them), is the one that receives the most attention.

→ *Colourful ticks:* A variation of funny money, is you give each person in the room some flipchart pens and a 'quota' of ticks, let's say 20 max, and then ask them to go around ticking the ideas they find most intriguing. So, if you end up giving a single idea 10 ticks, you think it's got huge potential, but if you only give an idea 1 tick, you think it's OKish. Then add the ticks up in a similar way, until you have found your eventual 'winner'.

## 2 CHECK

Check that you're not getting too carried away too quickly, or 'Hold your horses', as they say in the movies. The chances are that your idea is still in its infancy, so it will need to be thought through and continually refined and polished before it's even close to ready.

Even if you're convinced you've already come up with an amazing idea, whatever you do, don't be too precious about it. If it's success you're after, you may need to tweak it a little (or perhaps a lot) to achieve the desired effect. By all means believe in your new idea, but don't become a prisoner of it. Put your pride to one side, and see your idea as a work in progress. This is because evidence suggests that our first idea, or first draft of our idea, may not necessarily be the best. Here are just a few examples to support this view…

→ Sherlock Holmes was originally called Sherringford Holmes

→ Joseph Heller's book *Catch-22* was originally called *Catch-18*

→ Ian Fleming's *Live and Let Die* was originally called *The Undertaker's Wind*

→ The hit TV show *Friends* was originally going to be called *Across the Hall*, and then even *Insomnia Café* was considered

→ The song 'Don't cry for me Argentina' was originally going to be called 'It's only your lover returning'.

## 3 CYCLE

Virtually all new ideas need 'help' if they're to flourish and prosper. Even Otto Rohwedder – the man who invented sliced bread – had to work hard for 17 years to help make this idea a reality, and even then it needed the help of marketers to sell it because no one wanted to buy it in the shops. The following technique is something I call the **The S.O.S. technique** because it aims to do precisely this.

The way it works is simple. All you have to do is take your new idea and then continually feed it around a 3-stage process...

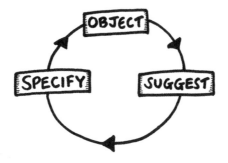

**Specify** what you have in mind and what's great about the idea

**Object** to what you *don't* think is great about the idea

**Suggest** a solution for getting beyond each objection.

And that's all there is to it really: **Specify... Object... Suggest. Specify... Object... Suggest.**

So, for example, supposing you're an entrepreneur who's just come up with an idea for making 'diamond umbrellas'.

You **Specify** that this is what you have in mind and that you like it because it's different and it will appeal to people with more money than sense, etc... As you think it over, however, you suddenly begin to have second thoughts. Your first key **Objection** is that it'd be too expensive to produce. So what do you do? Ditch the idea?

No way (at least, not yet). Some of the best business ideas in history started off by being ridiculous ones...

Simply take the same idea into the **Suggest** phase, and then explore potential ways of producing diamond umbrellas 'inexpensively'.

For example, you might consider using cheaper diamonds, diamond substitutes, or perhaps you might even get away from the idea of real diamonds altogether, and think instead of umbrellas in the shape of a diamond, an umbrella with pictures of diamonds on them, or manufacturing umbrellas that are able to shine like diamonds… and so on.

So, instead of giving up at the **Objection** phase by thinking, 'But nobody will want to buy diamond umbrellas', turn your **Objection** into a new question like, 'In what ways could I create diamond umbrellas that people really would want to buy?' This will help provoke and inspire new suggestions. For example, what if you could make umbrellas as strong as diamonds, so they don't break in a forceful wind? Or children's umbrellas that play 'Twinkle Twinkle Little Star'… well, you know what I mean. **S.O.S.**

# S.O.S.

## S.O.S. CASE STUDY

A few years ago a TV and film producer I know called Andy Harries was having a meeting about a new series of *Prime Suspect* – a UK police detective drama starring Helen Mirren. During the meeting he noticed how everyone was making a real fuss of the actress, making sure she was happy with everything from the tea she was drinking to the seat she was sitting on. In fact, he noticed that people were treating her with such reverence, it was almost as if she was the Queen. Suddenly, he had one of those light-bulb moments, or what we refer to as **Specify**: 'How about we cast Helen Mirren in a movie as Queen Elizabeth II? Who knows, with a bit of make-up here and there, it's possible, and, because people the world over love the Queen, we could be on to a winner.' The moment he left the meeting, he got straight on the phone to a screenwriter friend of his and a film director friend of his to explore the concept.

However, as we discussed earlier, after the initial buzz of the idea, this is usually where the *buts* come in, such as, 'But the Queen's been on the throne for over 40 years. How on earth can we condense that into a two-hour movie?' Clearly they could have stopped there and then, and thrown the idea in the bin. But they didn't. They used this **Objection** to help improve the idea, by **Suggesting**, 'What if we didn't focus on all of her reign? How about we only focus on one part her reign instead?' And so, the **S.O.S.** process continued, with each new **Objection** being used to stimulate a fresh **Suggestion**.

> 'But a year's still too long.'
>
> 'OK, how about we focus on only one week instead?'
>
> 'But which week?'
>
> 'How about the week of Diana's death?'
>
> 'But that'll be too controversial.'
>
> 'OK, how about we make it less controversial, by seeing Diana's death from the Queen's perspective instead...'

Then, of course, they still had to make the film, and promote it.

The reason for mentioning this is twofold. Firstly, it is important to realise that coming up with a great idea is only a single part of the creative process, not all of it. Clearly *The Queen* might never have ended up being the success it was – with numerous Oscar nominations – if it hadn't been continually improved and refined. Secondly, however, it is to show how the best way to 'bulletproof' an idea is to use **Objections**, rather than do what most of us do and shy away from them.

# 4 CLIMB

As we all know, coming up with clever ideas is one thing. Actually turning them into reality is another. And what is it that invariably stops most ideas from ever seeing the light of day? *Fear*. Fear of what other people might think, fear of what other people might say, fear of what other people might do…

Of course, sometimes this fear is perfectly justified, and sometimes the critics turn out to be right. Let's face it, even a broken watch tells the right time twice a day.

Plenty of new business ideas have fallen flat on their face, and famous examples like New Coke and the Sinclair C5 are only two.

Having said this, however, it doesn't take a genius to realise that, if cynics were allowed to rule the world, few of the creative achievements we enjoy so much today would ever have happened, such as…

→ *The Eiffel Tower*… 'But Paris is a low city, and a tower of this kind will be out of keeping with it.'

→ *The Beatles*… 'But there's no future for guitar bands.'

→ *Pirates of the Caribbean*… 'But audiences don't want swashbuckling movies any more.'

→ *FedEx*… 'But who's going to pay for an overnight postal service when they can use the U.S. mail instead?'

→ *The microscope* – invented by Zacharias Jansen in 1590 – 'But who on earth wants to look at small things?'

It has to be said, however, that often the harshest critic of our ideas is not other people, but ourself. Some experts even believe that 87 per cent of self-talk (the way we communicate with ourselves within our heads) is negative.

In this respect it is vital that we learn strategies for tackling our inner critic, gremlin or whatever else you want to call it, otherwise we run the risk of living a life half-lived.

Here are a couple you might find useful.

## a) FORGET ABOUT BEING PERFECT

Nobody's perfect, all of the time. We're all FHB (fallible human beings). Once we accept this, life can become a whole lot easier. Of course it's good to have high standards and to aim high, but if we base our entire self-worth on the results we do or do not achieve, we will wrongly assume that, if we fail, we are a failure. This is simply not true. Psychologists tell us that failure is an end result. Failing, however, is different. It's possible to fail again and again, but eventually succeed, as long as we keep learning something new each time we fail. Many of the most successful people in business have failed on numerous occasions – from Edison to Disney – but because they've kept going and continually adapted their approach, they have eventually managed to achieve their desired outcome.

Bear in mind that 'rigid perfectionists' are often their own worst enemy. They rarely complete projects or achieve success because they never stop adding the 'finishing touches' to their work, and because they live in constant fear of being criticised. Nobody likes being criticised, but think about it. What's the alternative?

## 'To avoid criticism, do nothing, say nothing, be nothing.'
Elbert Hubbard

## b) FOCUS ON WHAT YOU CAN DO, NOT ON WHAT YOU CAN'T

It's very easy sometimes – when being creative – to feel defeated, deflated and helpless when the odds are against us. 'What's the point?' we might say to ourselves. 'Yeah sure, I can be as creative as I like, but what difference is it going to make?' This might be particularly apt if you happen to work in an organisation where 'the powers that be' are far from receptive to new ideas.

If this rings true for you, however, please don't give up. Keep reminding yourself, that sometimes – with a little imagination – it really is possible for the tail to wag the dog. As the boy David proved when he defeated the giant Goliath, what matters at the end of the day is not creativity itself but *creative leverage*...

So use the tools in this book not only to help you generate new ideas, but also to help promote and sell your ideas, too.

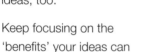

Keep focusing on the 'benefits' your ideas can bring to others, and what it is that *they* want (rather than *you* want), and the chances are you'll soon find you're able to achieve a great deal more by doing a great deal less...

# CONCLUSION

Throughout this book we have explored the world of **Genius** and how **Cunningly Clever Creativity** can potentially help you to achieve outstanding results in both your personal and professional life.

If there's one thing you take away from reading it, however, I hope it is this.

**Cunningly Clever Creativity** is not just a practical 'creative thinking' toolbox. Above all else, it is an attitude of mind. It is a particular way of looking at the world.

For example, in the eyes of some people, the following symbol is just a full stop, and it always will be.

For a **Cunningly Clever Creative**, however, the same dot could be perceived as a beginning rather than an ending, and perhaps even the difference between failure and success…

## 'Every wall is a door'
Ralph Waldo Emerson

# FURTHER INFORMATION

If you're genuinely interested in **Genius** and the world of creative thinking and would like to find out more, I recommend you read a variety of books and articles by the following authors/ organisations to help you on your quest…

# AND FINALLY...

You might also want to visit **www.geniusthinking.co.uk** or **www.jamesbannerman.com** to explore a wide range of business consulting, training and coaching services for helping you to boost your personal and professional success.

www.geniusthinking.co.uk

www.jamesbannerman.com

**'The voyage of discovery lies not in seeking new horizons, but in seeing with new eyes.'**
Marcel Proust

# Read on

9780273767701

"*The Procrastination Equation* is crammed with surprising insights about procrastination and human nature – as well as concrete, helpful solutions for fighting procrastination."

- **Gretchen Rubin**, author of *The Happiness Project*

"*The Procrastination Equation* will teach you how to bust the excuses that are preventing you from doing your best work and living your best life. So don't put it off any longer. Read this book. Today."

- **Daniel Pink**, author of *Drive and A Whole New Mind*

# Don't be good. Be brilliant.

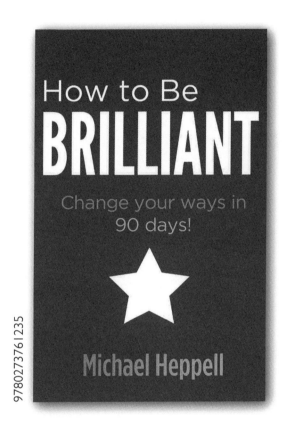